Live, Work and Play
in Australia

Live, Work and Play in Australia

Sharyn McCullum

Kangaroo Press

The author has tried her utmost to make sure the information is the latest available, but things can change, and neither she nor the publisher can take responsibility for this.

To keep the information up-to-date the author travels regularly plus uses her established network of contacts throughout Australia and around the world.

She is happy to receive information from readers to improve the guide for future fellow travellers

Send any correspondence to:
PO Box 346
Gymea NSW 2227
Australia

The author would like to thank all those people who gave their time and knowledge freely, and even those who felt the extraction of information was like having a tooth pulled.

Special thanks to:
Dearne Alcorn
Caroline Smith
Mark Taylor
Malcolm and Diane Simister

© Sharyn McCullum 1996

First published in 1996 by Kangaroo Press Pty Ltd
3 Whitehall Road Kenthurst NSW 2156 Australia
P.O. Box 6125 Dural Delivery Centre NSW 2158
Printed by Australian Print Group, Maryborough VIC 3465

ISBN 086417 773 9

Contents

1 **Introduction** 9

2 **Organise yourself before you go** 10
   Can you go — Passport and working holiday visa 10
   When to go 11
   How to go 14
   Packing 15
   The question of money 22
   Sorting affairs 23
   Holiday insurance and medical care 24
   Things to do 26
   Mail holding/advisory services 28
   Electronic voice mail services 30
   Useful publications and information 31
   Checklist 33
   Travelling alone 34
   Travelling safe 35
   Travelling well 37

3 **Arriving** 39
   By sea vessel 39
   By plane 39
   Arriving at Sydney Airport 40
   Transport from Sydney Airport 41
   Arriving at other airports 42

4 **Now you've arrived** 43
   Open a bank account 43
   Tax File Number 44
   Register Medicare 44
   Where to start 45

5   Accommodation 47
    Short-term accommodation 47
    Hostels, camping/caravan parks, B&B, Farm Stays 47
    Long-term accommodation 52
    Renting a flat/house 52
    Living in Sydney 55
    Living in other areas 56

6   Work opportunities 57
    Working & studying 58
    Working in Sydney and the rest of NSW 59
    Working in other states 59
    Finding work 60
    What is taken from your salary 65
    Accounting 66
    Agriculture 69
    Au Pair work 75
    Banking, finance and stockbroking 76
    Bars 77
    Buskers 78
    Charity collecting 78
    Child/elder carers 79
    Computer contracting 80
    Customer sourcing 82
    Deck hand/cook 82
    Diving instructors 84
    Farm/station work 85
    Hospitality 87
    Journalism and photography 89
    Legal 90
    Nursing 91
    Office support 95
    Resort work 99
    Roadhouses 102
    Scientific/lab staff 102
    Teaching 103
    Technical, industrial, trades and unskilled work 104
    Travel consultants 105
    Waiting 106

7   Holidaying 107

Sightseeing Sydney 107
Transport around Sydney 107
Hitting Sydney's tourist spots — a suggestion 110
Sightseeing the rest of Australia 114
Travel options 116
Suggested routes 128

8   Useful information 140

Aboriginal Australia; ANZAC Day; Aussie tucker; backpacker scene; bank opening times; barbecues; blue/bluey; bushfires; bushrangers; clothes; currency; cyclones; dates; deadliest creatures; departure tax; drinking; driving; eating out; eucalyptus oil; emergency numbers; fauna; flies; gay scene; heat and humidity; lingo; luggage storage; metric; newspaper; nightlife; outdoors; politics/government; post; public holidays; radio; religions; shopping; smoking; sunburn; skin cancer; social events for the calendar; Southern Cross; sporting mad; surf and turf; tax; telephone system; time zones; tipping; TV; water; visa; weather; World Heritage-listed areas

Index 158

1 Introduction

It has become the norm for today's generation to take time out to live and work overseas, and a popular destination to do this is Australia.

You don't have to be a gregarious child of adventure either. All you need is a passport, a visa, a desire to experience a new culture, the will to take any work available and a penchant for a good time—well, that's my theory anyway!

Unfortunately many arrive and find themselves with no friends, no family, no work, nowhere to live and wondering: What do I do now?

Hopefully this won't be you because with a little pre-planning and knowledge of available opportunities any worries should be minimal and probably covered by the following tips.

There are various visas available for those wishing to experience the land down-under, but this guide is primarily written for those arriving on the one-year **working holiday visa.** Whether you're arriving as a visitor, a student (see the separate section under **Study Options**) or a migrant you will still find plenty of useful and pertinent information.

It is up to you how and where you spend your time in Australia, but many working holidaymakers make Sydney their base for 6–9 months and then travel for 3–6 months. This is usually because Sydney is where the plane touches down and where there is a concentration of jobs. A lot of information is centred around Sydney for these reasons.

For those who go against this norm, I've included as many work opportunities as possible so you can work your way around the country.

Whatever the motivation behind your working holiday, read on and enjoy your time in Australia!

2 Organise yourself before you go

Can you go?

You will need a fully valid **passport** to enter Australia. If you don't have one you had better get yourself one.

If you do have one, check the expiry date to confirm that it is valid for your entire stay. Applying for a new passport in a foreign country is one hassle you can do without.

Everyone who comes to Australia must have a visa. There are various types available, but this guide is specifically written for those arriving on the working holiday visa.

Working holiday visa

Australia has working holiday visa arrangements with the United Kingdom, the Republic of Ireland, the Netherlands, Canada, Japan and Korea for those aged 18 to 25 and 11 months. This list is being extended to include Greece, Italy, Spain, France and Germany.

If you are from a non-arrangement country, or aged 26 to 30 and 11 months, you are still welcome to apply, but along with your application you must submit a statement explaining how a visit by you to Australia will be of benefit to you and Australia. What you say in this statement will be taken into account when your visa approval is being considered.

Please note that some travellers who are hoping to obtain teaching or nursing work will be required to pass a medical examination.

There are some stipulations you should be aware of when you obtain the visa: your main reason is to have a holiday; you need to be single or married without children; have the equivalent of around A$5,000 in a bank account; have a return airfare or enough money to buy one; have a good chance of finding temporary work to supplement your holiday funds; confirm that you don't intend to enrol for formal studies and will depart at the end of your stay.

You can request the application form at any time, though it is advised not to apply for the visa until 4–5 weeks before you hope to travel. You might want to read the next section, 'When to Go?', to help decide this.

The visa is valid for 13 months from the date of issue. If you apply on July 1, 1996 it is valid till August 1, 1997. The extra month gives you time to prepare for your trip and still allows you the maximum of a 12-month stay. If you take a little longer to arrive in Australia because you are visiting other places first, you can apply for an extension to take you up to the 12 months. There is a cost for this and the success of your application depends on the officials in Australia. It may be an idea to plan your extra travels after your stay in Australia.

Those from the UK, Ireland, the Netherlands and Canada can apply for a visa at any **Australian Consulate** or **High Commission**, so you could undertake other travels before your arrival. Those from Japan, Korea and other European countries should apply in their own country of citizenship.

Apply in person at your nearest visa-issuing Australian High Commission or Consulate, taking with you your application, application fee and bank statement.

Some travel agents can lodge an application form for you. It usually takes a week or so to be approved but for those in London aged 18 to 25 and 11 months, the visa is usually issued on the spot.

As visa requirements can change you are advised to get the latest details from your nearest Australian Consulate or High Commission.

When to go?

Some people can throw caution to the wind and jump on a plane to Australia without hesitation, while others plan every minute detail months in advance. The influencing factors in deciding when to go include the weather, the cost of airfares and accommodation, the availability of work opportunities and the possibility of attending special events.

The weather and prime times to travel
Someone said to me 'I come from a country that has some of the coldest winters in the world—if I can follow the sun and avoid a winter, then I'm gonna.'

It is possible to have a year-round summer if that's what you want. Simply stay in the southern states during the summer months, then head north during the winter months. So when to arrive in Australia?

Any time really. As for travelling the country, there are prime times for seeing some sights. For instance the outback and the Great Barrier Reef are far better during the winter months.

Unlike most northern hemisphere countries where the further north you travel the colder it becomes, Australia is the opposite. The further north you travel the hotter it becomes. During the summer months (remember the seasons in the southern hemisphere are opposite to those in the northern hemisphere) the weather can be very uncomfortable for the traveller who is not used to it.

A big influence on the northern half of Australia is the Tropic of Capricorn, which runs through it. This gives the top half two seasons; wet and dry.

During the wet season (November to April) days are hot and humid with a lot of rain and usually a cyclone or two around the coast. The stingers (jellyfish) are also out in force in the ocean.

You can still visit the area during this time, after all many Australians live there, but you will encounter more rain and hotter days with high humidity which many travellers find uncomfortable. If your plan is to laze on a beach in Queensland during this time you may be a little disappointed. Or if you want to experience the outback you might find it too excruciatingly hot to enjoy.

During the winter months in the north the weather is more pleasant. There is less rain if you want to lie on a beach, and outback days are warm and dry with cool evenings. Not many people realise that the desert areas do become cool during the dry winter season but the desert is like a cold-blooded animal; it doesn't retain its heat when the sun goes down.

The bottom half of the country—New South Wales, Victoria, Tasmania, South Australia and the bottom half of Western Australia—has four quite distinct seasons. It can be very cold during winter with snow appearing in the mountains and during summer there are long, hot and humid days. Cool changes are often prayed for to lower the temperature. Many a day is spent on the coastline lapping up the sun.

If you want to see the sights in prime times, stay south during the summer months then head north for winter. Remember though that many working holidaymakers will travel during prime time, and backpacker accommodation can be scarce.

Airfares and accommodation

These are high on the priority list as their cost can influence when to go. There are high, low and shoulder season airfares. Of course airfares are most expensive during the high season.

The high season is December to February (Oz summer time). The low season is April to August, which is the end of autumn and all of winter, while the shoulder seasons are autumn and spring. The difference in price from high to low can be a few hundred dollars. In backpacker terms this can mean a couple of weeks' hostel accommodation. The high season can begin at any time in December and end at any time in February, so check with your travel agent.

Some prefer to leave as close as possible to the end of the low season to take advantage of a cheaper airfare, but arrive at the beginning of the next season. If you are going to travel during the low season, book early, as many people—especially those who have just read this—could be looking to do so as well.

Also book early if you are looking to arrive in December as you will be vying for bum-space with many Australians returning home for Christmas after their jaunts around the world.

Prices for short-term accommodation (camping, hotels, holiday flats, etc.) increase and sometimes double during school holidays, especially over Christmas and New Year when families take their holidays. Hostel prices usually remain constant (though some places can increase their rates during holiday periods). You may need to book in advance as during the busy times you might not secure a bed if you leave it till the last minute.

Sometimes the importance of seeing a particular place in the best weather conditions or attending a special event should take precedence over factors like the cost of airfare and accommodation. Is a saving of A$200 worth it if you miss out on something you really want to see?

Work opportunities

Just as the weather can influence your travel plans, so might the availability of work opportunities. Under the various headings in the section on **Work Opportunities**, I have tried to indicate the busy and quiet times. Those heading to Sydney for the Christmas and New Year period (which many do to attend Christmas Day celebrations on Bondi Beach), should try to be there around November because not only are you vying for positions with other backpackers, but with university students who have a 3-month summer vacation and with school students who have a 6-week summer break.

Overall, work is available year-round though some times are busier than others.

Particular events

The timing of a particular event you wish to see may influence your decision on when to go or when to travel; for instance: Would you like to go whale watching in Hervey Bay? Would you like to see a cricket match or a game of one of the three football codes? Would you like to see the Sydney Harbour Bridge lit up with fireworks on New Year's

Eve? Do you want to go to the Gay and Lesbian Mardi Gras? Would you like to attend the Melbourne Cup, which stops the nation for three minutes every year? (See **Useful Information** for a listing of major events.)

How to go?

As Australia is surrounded by various oceans and seas there are really only two ways to reach its distant shores. Sailing, which can take several weeks, and of course, the most popular and quickest method, flying.

Sailing isn't as popular these days as it once was but many ocean vessels visit Australia's shores. You could arrive as a freighter passenger or on an ocean liner; perhaps as crew on a private yacht or freighter.

There are many airlines flying into Australia, which means Australia can be part of a world tour or can be visited on its own.

Depending on the route chosen, your flight can take a few ice-filled drinks, wrestles with packets of peanuts, a dinner, a light refreshment, a breakfast, hopefully a snooze, a couple of trips to the loo and a movie or two. But how many hours? Well, from the UK and Europe between 24 to 36 hours. From North America between 14 to 25 hours. From Japan about 12 hours. From New Zealand about three hours. From Africa, Asia and South America about 10 to 15 hours.

Many like to break the long trip with a stop-over, which those who suffer from sinus problems might appreciate, as exposure to long periods of cabin air can cause the nose to become dried out and stuffy. In my case a long flight can make my nose bleed—you really wanted to know that, didn't you?—but it happens to a lot of people. People who wear contacts might want to wear glasses for a long flight as the cabin air can dry your eyes. A stop-over might also help alleviate jetlag and any other effects associated with flying, like swollen ankles.

Smokers might also like a stop-over as some airlines flying to Australia are non-smoking. If you can't survive for more than a few hours without a nicotine fix then find an airline which allows smoking, or has regular stops.

Following are some possible routes to Australia:

From UK/Europe: USA/Canada island-hop Pacific; Trans-Siberian then fly/sail; Overland Middle Asia then fly/sail; Overland Africa then fly/sail; Fly to Asia, overland Asia (island-hop) and fly/sail to Darwin.

From North America: Overland to South America then fly/sail; Pacific Island stop-over; New Zealand stop-over.

From Asia: Island-hop Indonesia to Darwin

There are different tickets available which are valid for a year, such as a round-the-world ticket, though if you are hoping to spend a full year in Australia this ticket might not be the one for you. You might want to enquire about 'open jaw' tickets where you can fly into one city and out of another.

Australia's international gateways are Sydney, Melbourne, Brisbane, Darwin, Cairns, Perth and Adelaide. Therefore you could fly into Perth, travel overland to Sydney for a flight out, or fly into Sydney and out of Darwin or Cairns. The choice is yours.

The most popular arrival destination is Sydney. If you plan to arrive there, you might wish to request a window seat on the left side of the plane because most planes approach the airport from a northerly direction, which means you will fly in over the city and receive a superb bird's-eye view of the Harbour Bridge and the Opera House. If your seat is on the right side don't worry, as you will see the sprawling metropolis of Sydney reaching the Great Dividing Range in the distance.

Sydney airport has become congested due to its popularity, so expect a wait through immigration and customs (as can be the case in many airports around the world), or maybe arrive in another city. An hour's wait can be annoying at the time but is soon forgotten.

Though we all like a bargain, remember that cheap flights aren't always the best. Sometimes there are restrictions; there might be five stop-overs before arrival in Australia, or they only arrive once or twice a week, which means you will have to fit your plans in around them. If you don't mind, then go with that airline but do shop around to find a ticket that suits you.

Travel agencies to look out for include:

STA that has over 100 branches in 50 cities and 11 countries. STA also have Q Travel designed for gays and lesbians.

YHA has travel offices all over the world. Look in your telephone book for the one closest to you. See the **Holidaying** section for details of the main offices in Australia.

Also look out for **Trailfinders**, **Campus Travel**, **Austravel** and **USIT**. Don't forget the big companies like **American Express**, **Harvey World Travel** and **Thomas Cook** and the small **bucket shops**.

There are many possibilities, so haunt travel agents and watch out for specials listed in papers until you find something that suits you, your aspirations and your budget.

Packing

Packing is an arduous task at the best of times; trying to squeeze in everything you think you will need for an extended stay in Australia can be horrendous.

There could be some of you who imagine that all you'll need to pack is swim wear, a towel for the beach, a pair of shorts and walking shoes for the outback. For those following the sun this might be all you need, but weather can change and Australia *does* have cold weather.

Before you begin to pack ask yourself: what kind of travelling will you be doing? For how long? Once you've answered these questions you will be able to choose the type of luggage that suits you. No matter what kind of travel you will be doing, you will want your luggage to be easily manouvred in and out of your transport, and easy to carry around. A **backpack** is far easier to carry around than a suitcase, especially if you happen to be walking in the red dirt of the outback.

There are various designs available so spend some time seeing what they offer. Some are top opening, while others have zippers. I prefer packs with zippers as I've seen people with top opening ones having to dig deep, or unpack their other belongings, to find what they are looking for. Those with zippers can also be locked. Try backpacks on and get the right size for your back length. If you decide to stick with a suitcase invest in a trolley.

You will also need a small **daypack** or **carry bag** to hold your camera, walkman, diary etc. This could also double as luggage for overnight or weekend trips, so take that into consideration when choosing. Some backpacks do come with a zip-off daypack and removable toiletries bag.

Don't forget to label your luggage inside and out and keep it locked. Make it stand out by tying ribbon on it, so you'll recognise it on sight.

Once you have your luggage you can consider what to pack. Ask yourself these questions before you do: How can I avoid looking like a tourist? Am I travelling to other countries before I arrive in Australia? Will these countries have dress regulations? When am I arriving in Australia? Summer or winter? I'm hoping to work in Australia, what type of work will it be?

OK, so how not to look like a tourist. Being a tourist can attract professional thieves, so try and blend in. It is hard not to be seen at some stage with your luggage, but try and find a place to store it as soon as possible.

I have heard people say: 'I dress down because people seem to leave me alone that way.' I have found this comment true in my travels and you too can take this into consideration when packing. Don't dress like you have loads of money and don't wear the family jewels or you'll stand out from the casually dressed Australians.

Australians do like to advertise where they have been on their travels, so try to wear t-shirts stating where you've been yourself and even where you're from. Other popular t-shirts to wear include those with surf brand names on them. If you blend in, some tourist just might ask you for directions!

Australia doesn't have any religious restrictions influencing dress, but if you are travelling to other countries before or after your Australian visit find out whether these countries have dress regulations. For instance, women travelling through the Middle East might need to cover their legs, at least.

You will need to pack for all types of weather in Australia. You'll need swim wear, shorts and t-shirts for the warm weather. Loose fitting clothes are best in hot weather and it's possible you'll make a few changes during the day. When it gets cold, especially in the southern states, you will need winter woollies and possibly an overcoat.

For work you will need suitable clothes. Under each work opportunity I have tried to include the clothes you are required to wear and any utensils you are expected to bring.

You might need a jumper or cardigan for indoors during summer, which probably sounds ridiculous to you now, but the hotter it is outside, the colder it can be indoors. Sometimes it can be too cold. But there is nothing like that 'Ahhhh' sensation you'll feel when you walk through the automatic doors to a gush of tingling coolness after being in the heat.

Going away usually means you want to buy new things to take with you. This can deplete your savings for your trip. When travelling, old clothes are just as useful and often preferable. Sometimes on a two or three day camping trip you might spend days in the same clothes, and in the outback the red dirt can get into everything—permenantly.

The travelling backpackers' uniform is shorts, t-shirt and sandals during the day, and for going out, jeans and a t-shirt or a loose fitting dress, and shoes.

Second hand stores are good places to look for cheap clothing. You can always buy things in Australia—many have commented that clothing in Australia is more expensive than at home but of course, it can depend on where you shop.

For compact travel items and knick-knacks, look in disposal and camping stores, bric-a-brac stores, travel agents, bag shops, specialist outdoor stores and YHA travel shops.

All the following suggestions are just that; suggestions. Makeshift, already acquired, or borrowed items will do the job just as effectively as new items. A lot of things can be bought in Australia when you need them, so even though it's nice to have new things to take away, save your money for your travels. I've highlighted with ** those items which can be readily bought in Australia.

Suggestions

Underwear ** Maybe a week or two's worth, as you don't know when you'll be able to wash it while travelling, but it is up to you. Maybe you want to hang free and loose. Cotton garments that breathe in the heat are highly recommended.

Swimwear ** Guys usually wear scungies (see 'lingo' in **Useful Information**) or board shorts. Girls wear bikinis and one-piece suits. You may wish to have a couple of pairs if you are planning to spend a lot of time in the sun—after all, you don't want to be seen in the same swimwear day after day! Swimwear can usually be bought all year round, especially in the northern states.

T-shirts ** A couple should do you—one off and one on, though in really hot weather you might make a couple of changes during the day.

Shorts ** One or two casual pairs to wear to the beach and for sightseeing plus a good pair for going out. Yes—during hot summer nights dressy shorts are worn out.

Hat ** With a wide brim to keep the sun off the back of your neck and face. Raffia hats are popular for girls and easily available. Baseball caps are also popular.

Sunglasses ** It is advisable to wear these at all times when outside, as a lot of eye diseases are related to over exposure to ultra-violet rays. Try to get a pair that also protects the side of your eyes.

Suntan lotion ** It is advised to wear SPF15+ unless you're after the lobster look. Bottles/tubes can be bought easily in chemists, supermarkets and shops near the beaches. Try and wear moisturisers with sun block already in them for added protection.

After sun cream **

Towel/s ** One that can double as a beach towel and a shower towel. I've seen a new-fangled one in camping stores which takes up less room than a towel and works like a shammy. I have heard varying reports about them.

Hand towel Good to take on long journeys when you need to freshen up. It feels much better than paper towel or toilet paper.

Walking shoes/hiking boots/joggers Wear them in before you leave home so you don't get blisters. You might want to spend a little extra for a good quality pair.

Socks A few pairs.

Thongs/Jandals/sandals ** Very good for wearing to the beach and sightseeing. Some travellers prefer a pair of good soled sandals to walking boots to let feet breathe. Saves washing socks too. Also good for wearing to the toilet and shower blocks at camp sites and hostels. If it gets cold you could wear a pair of socks with your sandals, but only if you don't mind looking like a tourist.

Leggings/track pants/sweat pants One or two pairs for cooler weather.
Jeans One or two pairs which can be worn casually or dressed up.
Jumper/sweater/jersey One or two, but try not to bring really bulky ones. You could buy a lambswool one in Australia.
Going-out shoes One pair, though if you have dressy sandals these can be worn. During summer, shoes that let your feet breathe are much better to wear than closed-in shoes. When you're sharing a hostel room, non-smelly feet are appreciated.
Going-out outfit One or two.
Work clothes See the **Work Opportunities** section.
Coat*** Can be bulky to carry but will be welcomed in the southern states during winter. A hooded water-proof jacket is preferable.
Gloves*** Handy for winter. You might need fingerless ones for fruit picking during winter.
Snow gear*** Can be easily rented in the ski fields or in city shops. You will find a lot of surf-and-ski shops—surfing for the summer and skiing for the winter.
Sleeping sheet/bag*** Very handy for dossing on floors, camping and staying in hostels. Hostels will rent out sheets to you if you don't have any and usually supply blankets. On camping trips a sleeping bag will come in handy, though most tour companies will hire these if you request it when booking.

Sleeping bags vary in quality and the degree of insulation they provide. When you're camping in the outback during winter (the most pleasant time to go) it can become very cool at night, reaching single Celsius figures (less than 50°F).

Money belt*** Apart from being uncomfortable and making one look as if pregnant or has a beer gut, these are a safe way to carry money, travellers' cheques and tickets, etc. Different styles exist; some you can wear around the neck or shoulder, similar to a gun holster. Check them out and see what suits you.
Torch*** You will be surprised how often comes in handy.
Travel clothes line and pegs*** It's hard to find a clothes hoist when you need one. You'll find these handy during your travels, though camp sites and hostels usually have a launderette with a washer and a dryer.
Washing powder*** I've seen small tubes of liquid wash at large supermarkets and some travel agents. Most hostels/camping grounds will supply a cup for between 20 to 50 cents via a machine or office attendant.
Plastic bags To hold dirty washing plus other bits and pieces.
Walkman/Discman and favourite tapes/CDs*** Preferably leave tape and CD covers behind to save space. Tapes are useful on organised bus tours, as drivers call for music to be played while driving to accompany the landscape passing by.

Camera/film ** You might wish to purchase these duty-free or buy a cheap disposable camera, available from chemists and supermarkets.

Travel iron Handy for clothes that need ironing, like work clothes. You could invest in an iron when you arrive and sell it when you move on. Many backpackers do wear the crumpled look while travelling. Some laundries have irons available.

Coathangers A couple are useful if staying put for a while.

Travel clock You don't want to be late for work now do you? If yours has a loud tick, don't pack it in your luggage as it could be mistaken for a bomb.

Power point adaptor Duty-free shops carry sets of plugs for Australia. Plugs have three prongs so if you're bringing a travel iron, hair dryer or shaver this will be very useful.

Blow-up neck pillow For those long journeys when you might need to sleep sitting up.

Foldaway umbrella ** For those times you get caught in the rain. It's also useful for taking down to the beach as it protects your skin from the sun.

Passport photos **

Swiss Army knife **

Needle, thread and scissors Only take small scissors so you don't set off any metal detector alarms at airports—it's embarrassing.

Roll-on insect repellent ** Mozzies, flies and other insects are a pain.

Toiletries ** Bring travel-size, like roll-on deodorant instead of a large can, or two-in-one shampoo and conditioner. Collect the free sachets from magazines. You can always change brands once you've arrived.

Toiletry bag Preferably water-proof for when you take it to the shower. Look for one with handles so you can hang it up.

Plug (one size fits all) ** If you like to shave or wash your face in a basin, as not all hostels or camping grounds provide them in shower blocks.

Toilet roll ** A very good idea when travelling in the outback and camping. Sometimes the bush is preferable to a public toilet!

CV (curriculum vitae) and references An updated, typed CV and references are essential if you want to obtain work.

Travel diary For all those wonderful memories.

Address book To keep in contact with old friends and to add new ones. Take two because this is one of the most commonly lost items.

Maps ** Essential for finding your way around. There are extensive selections available in bookshops, service stations and newsagents. Information centres and hostels will have a free map of the local area. Motoring organisations provide free maps to members.

Writing material ** Pre-paid aerograms are available from post offices. Postcards are also available. Don't forget a pen.

Medicines Brands can differ in Australia. Some medications obtained over-the-counter back home may only be available on prescription in Australia. Obtain a supply to cover you for your stay and don't forget to have written permission from your doctor or health department just in case the drug is illegal in Australia or in other countries you will be travelling through.
*Multi-vitamins*** In case you drink too much and don't eat properly. Know your **blood group**.
*Condoms*** A necessity these days.
*Constipation/diarrhoea/upset tummy tablets*** Travelling can do weird things to the digestive system.
*Bandaids/plasters***
*Headache tablets***
*Sting relief*** When bitten by nasties.
*Antiseptic/healing cream*** For cuts and abrasions.
Travel sickness tablets If you're susceptible to it.
*Water purifying tablets/purifier*** If you're serious about your water. You could just drink the bottled stuff. Water is safe to drink in Oz, though the taste varies from area to area.
Flag Good for flying at sporting events.

OK, you've chosen luggage and gathered everything to take. Now lay it all out on the floor to see what you have. Go get a coffee or tea or your favourite potion then sit in front of your piles and consider why you're taking each item. Convince yourself of its worth or worthlessness. Finally, let's pack.

Everyone has a trick for packing. Some people stack things flat, but one way I find useful for backpacks is rolling clothes up tightly which seems to minimise wrinkles and lets me cram more in. I've also found that packing heavy objects in the middle, close to the back of the pack, will help keep the centre of gravity in the right place.

Keep useful accessories and things you'll be needing a lot near the top for easy access. Better still, keep them in your daypack.

Keep in mind any baggage allowances on organised trips and planes (usually 20 kg). I've noticed that some airlines now have a size and weight limit on cabin luggage so check this out with your travel agent.

To minimise weight, get rid of unnecessary packaging. Take new shirts and pantyhose out of boxes. A friend uses empty spice jars and film cases to carry enough toiletries to get to her destination. She also carries money and jewellery in them. I collect the sample sachets of shampoo and conditioner delivered through the post or given away free in magazines. I also request samples at make-up counters.

If you find you can't fit everything in or are over the 20 kg airline allowance and you believe you can't live without all your essentials, you might consider sending luggage as unaccompanied baggage. Ring your airline's cargo department and find out rates and procedures. But try to travel as light as possible—it makes life a lot easier.

Remember to keep something out to wear on the plane, something comfortable, loose fitting and suitable for the weather at your destination.

I would suggest you dress nicely when travelling by plane through Asian countries with strict drug regulations, as I have found that people who appear to be scruffy are often singled out to be searched.

You might wish to have some activities to do on the plane; books, music, games, a pack of cards. Check with the airline if you can use computers and CD players as they can interfere with navigation equipment.

The following items are often useful on the plane: an eye mask; socks to keep feet warm; ear plugs to keep out the engine hum; a face towel and toiletries to freshen up; a bottle of spray water to keep face moisturised; a neck rest; sinus tablets.

The question of money

How much to take

'The heaviest baggage for a traveller is an empty purse.' So take as much money as possible.

Throughout the guide I have tried to include prices which are correct at the time of publication, to give you an idea of costs. You will need to budget for expenses such as accommodation, food, sightseeing and spending money.

Some examples of costs are as follows:

Hostel accommodation	A$12–16 per night (look out for weekly rates)
Flat/house	A$100 per week for a room
Food	A$4–10 per meal
Beer	A$2 (varies from place to place)
Transport	See the **Holidaying** section

How to take it
Open a bank account in Australia from home and transfer funds over, or carry your funds on a credit card; it's the way to go.

Opening a bank account in Australia from your own country and transferring the funds over will save you the hassle of having to cash travellers' cheques and being charged commission. Also if you run out of money, more can easily be sent. Ask your bank if they can do this for you. If they can, request a savings account with an ATM (Automatic Teller Machine) card so that you can use an ATM. For security reasons the card won't be issued until you arrive, but the account can still be used if you go into the bank itself with ID. (See the section **Now you've arrived** for more information on Australian banks.)

These cards may also be used in some supermarkets, shops and petrol stations as many now offer **EFTPOS** (Electronic Funds Transfer at Point of Sale). You can also ask for cash if your card is accepted.

I have heard that various ATM cards from some countries are able to be used in Australia. Check with your bank to see if your current card can be used.

A credit card will be very useful. The most widely used cards are Mastercard and Visa though other cards are accepted. What many travellers do is credit their credit card, pay for goods and services with it, and when they need cash obtain a cash advance. You can obtain cash from ATMs wherever you see machines with the Mastercard and Visa signs, so make sure you have a PIN (Personal Identification Number).

Check the expiry date of your card and make sure it is valid for the entire length of your stay, because you don't want to be caught out. Make sure you take emergency contact numbers in case you lose it. Check with your bank about how to make payments from overseas.

These two methods are so much easier than worrying about finding a place to cash your travellers' cheques. Some places charge extortionate commission to cash them for you, especially in the outback. If you do take them, carry denominations of $50 or $100 in Australian dollars, as the commission is usually charged per cheque.

Thomas Cook and American Express travellers' cheques are the most popular and there are offices in Australia which will cash them without charging commission. Other places to exchange them include banks, tourist shops and major hotels. You will most likely have to produce your passport as ID to cash the cheques, while having a credit card and/or ATM access will save you having to carry your documents around.

Remember to keep a record of the serial numbers on your travellers' cheques. Stash this list separately from the cheques themselves, and leave a copy at at home in case they are lost or stolen.

Sorting affairs

Take the hassle out of paying bills at home by adding an extra signature to your bank account. This person will then be allowed to operate your account on your behalf. Make sure you leave enough in it so the bills can be paid, and money sent to you if the need arises.

You can also sign a **power of attorney**, giving a trusted friend, family member, professional person or body the authority to act on your behalf with regard to your affairs while you are away. The form can be obtained from legal stationers and some newsagents, and the arrangement is valid until revoked.

As Katherine Mansfield said: 'Whenever I prepare for a journey I prepare as though for death. Should I never return, all is in order. This is what life has taught me.'

Making a will might be unpleasant and sound absurd but it is a good idea. You are going away to enjoy yourself and sometimes you will do things you wouldn't normally do, like bungee jumping, diving a coastal wreck, rock climbing, bush walking or learning to surf—each having elements of danger to them.

Now I'm not saying the bungee rope will snap, or a shark will be lurking in the wreck, or you'll fall off a cliff or be bitten by a deadly snake in the bush, or be thrown off your surfboard by a whopper wave, but there is nothing worse than leaving your relatives to sort out the legal mess in the wake of your demise. Chances are slim that anything will happen to you, but you never know.

Holiday insurance and medical care

Holiday insurance is just that; insurance which covers you while you're on holiday, so if you plan on working check with your insurer whether this insurance is valid during periods of work (your employer should cover you while you're working). Not that you're expecting to hurt yourself on the job, but you might want to know who will cover medical bills, hospital costs, etc.

It is wise to shop around. Read the fine print on different policies, compare what they cover you for and how much they pay out if things do go wrong.

Trip cancellation, travel documents, medical expenses, luggage and personal effects, accidental death and personal liability are usually covered. Get your travel agent (they will usually refer you to the actual insurer) to go through it with you or make sure you read the fine print.

If you are taking expensive items like cameras, video equipment, computers, etc. you might wish to take out additional insurance as these aren't usually covered in general policies.

If you think you might participate in activities such as scuba diving, snow or water skiing, bungee jumping, parachuting or paragliding, check if you are covered. If not, you might want to cover yourself for such things. You can also take out more insurance in Australia.

Take emergency contact numbers in case something does happen. Should you need to put in a claim make sure you report your loss to someone in authority, like the police, the hotel owner, etc. Obtain a written statement from them to back up your story.

Remember, if you take out insurance, as a rule you cannot claim until you return to your own country. If however, you hold one of the following policies: Europeiska, Sweden; Europeiske Reiseforsikring A/S, Norway; Europaeiske Rejseforsikrings A/S, Denmark; Eurooppalainen Europeiska, Finland; Europeesche Verzekeringen, Holland; you don't have to wait until you get home. You can lodge a claim at:

Sydney Euro-Centre
Level 5, 200 George Street
Sydney NSW 2000
Tel: (02) 247 2700
Freecall for Australia outside Sydney: 1800 626 823

Australia has **reciprocal medical arrangements** with the United Kingdom, New Zealand, Sweden, the Netherlands, Finland, Malta and Italy. If you are from one of these countries you are covered for medical care in public hospitals through Medicare.

Travellers from the above countries often take out insurance that covers their travels to Australia, register at Medicare to cover them medically (this won't cover personal effects, etc), then take out more travel insurance in Australia to cover them for their travels within Australia.

If you want to know more about Medicare contact your health scheme as they should have a brochure available, or pop into an office after you arrive.

Vaccinations are not required to enter Australia as it is a low risk country, though it wouldn't hurt (no pun intended) to have childhood shots boosted, plus Hepatitis A, Polio and Tetanus. Have these shots about six weeks ahead of your departure in case you have any adverse reactions.

Australia does need to see a vaccination record if you are arriving from yellow fever areas (South America and Africa) within six days of being there.

If you live in a low risk country your body has not been exposed to many diseases and you may have a low level of immunity, so if you're travelling through a high risk country on your way to Australia, you are more susceptible to illnesses. Therefore, check with your doctor or a specialist in travel medicine for the correct shots. Also see if you require a vaccination record as some countries require you to have one before you may enter.

It is wise to have a **check-up** with a doctor or dentist before you leave as it is horrible being sick in a foreign country. While you're at the doctor obtain enough medication to last you for the duration of your stay as brands can differ in Australia. As I've said before, some drugs bought over-the-counter in other countries require a prescription in Australia and vice versa. If you do have prescribed drugs on you, carry a note from the prescribing doctor explaining what they are and for whom they have been prescribed.

Things to do

Pre-book accommodation. If you know when you're arriving in Australia you might wish to pre-book accommodation for at least a week, possibly two, after your arrival. I say this because by the time you have recovered from jetlag and done some sightseeing the week will be almost up. It is advisable to book if you are arriving during school holidays, especially the summer holiday which begins in mid-December and lasts until the end of January. See the **Accommodation** section for information on finding both short-term and long-term accommodation.

When you pre-book your accommodation ask if a complimentary pick-up from the airport is included and if not, find out how you can get to the place.

One reason to **pre-book your travel within Australia** is that some travel passes (namely air passes) are cheaper when they are bought outside Australia.

A reason not to pre-book is that when you get to Australia, you might find your pass isn't suitable for what you want to do anymore. Perhaps you've met the guy/girl of your dreams or some other travellers and want to change your plans.

There are air, train and bus passes available so I suggest you ask your travel agent about them. Also have them run through the conditions with you and find out what flexibility the passes offer—e.g. if you do change your mind in Australia can you re-route your ticket? If you don't want to use the pass can you obtain a refund?

Air passes are designed for travellers to Australia. Unlike Australians who usually require a return ticket, travellers are heading in one direction even though they might end up where they started.

Air passes include the **Explorer Pass, Discover Australia Pass** and the **Australian Airpass**. Check them out. They cannot be bought in Australia.

Bus passes are available overseas. The two largest companies in Australia are Greyhound Pioneer Australia and McCafferty's. Both offer good deals. Pick up their brochures and check them out. Bus Passes

Organise yourself before you go

available overseas can easily be obtained in Australia. (See the **Holidaying** section for more about them).

Train passes can be bought overseas and in Australia.

There are plenty of travel options available once you're in Australia. See the **Holidaying** section.

To pre-book or not to pre-book? This is a question only you can answer. By booking in advance you will know how much time and money you have left to play with.

Your national driver's licence is sufficient for short holiday stays in Australia though it is recommended you obtain an **International Driver's licence.** Some car rental companies prefer you to have one, and it is required if you buy a car.

If you plan to buy a car in Australia you can apply for a **CMC** (Commonwealth Motoring Card) from your motoring service that will allow you to receive reciprocal motoring help from Australia's associations. Make sure you bring proof of membership from your organisation.

As you probably know, joining the **Youth Hostels Association** enables you to take advantage of cheap accommodation offered all over the world and Australia is no exception. If you don't join in your own country, you can join in Australia. Being a YHA member also entitles you to a variety of discounts. Obtain the booklet when you join.

In competition with YHA are **BRA** (Backpacker Resorts of Australia) hostels. It is not necessary to join the organisation in order to stay at their hostels, but if you do so there is usually a A$1 discount. BRA can easily be joined in Australia (see the **Accommodation** section for more about them). Joining BRA qualifies you for a VIP card, allowing you to receive a range of discounts.

Collecting **air miles** has become very popular in Australia. The two largest associations in Australia, QANTAS and Ansett, have air mile or frequent flyer clubs of their own which are linked with many overseas airlines. You might want to join one of these clubs because just the long flight to Australia should accumulate a few points for you. Watch out for other schemes offering points.

If you are a full-time student you can apply for an **ISIC** card (International Student Identity Card). This card will enable you to receive discounts and special services worldwide.

Getting fit for your holiday—WHY?
Holidaying in Australia often involves outdoor activities, simple activities like sightseeing for instance. Do you want to climb Ayers Rock? (The Aboriginal name is Uluru.) It can take a couple of hours and is rather strenuous. If you don't climb it you can always walk around the base, just a mere 9 km. Do you want to learn to dive? You need to pass

a medical for that.

Other things you might like to try include renting a push bike, exploring caves, swimming at the beach or bush walking. There is plenty to do in Australia and if you're reasonably fit, you should be able to enjoy those things you want to do.

Those hoping to spend a lot of time on a beach often overdose in the first few days, so it might be an idea to prepare your skin by taking a few sessions under a **sunbed**.

It is likely you'll want to obtain **duty-free** items. You are permitted to bring in 1 litre of alcohol, 250 cigarettes, any reasonable amount of perfume as long as it's for personal use and A$400 worth of other goods. This amount is really for returning Aussies who may have to pay a duty on the goods. If you bring in a very expensive item like a camera, you shouldn't have to pay duty on it as long as you intend taking it out of the country with you when you go. Do bring ownership papers or a receipt with you.

Mail holding/advisory services

If you would like to leave people an address where they can contact you, you can use the old faithful **Poste Restante** or you could join one of the **mail holding/advisory services** below.

Australia Japan Working Holiday Advisory Office is a non-profit organisation set up purely as an advisory service for young Japanese on a working holiday in Australia. The service is very reputable and sponsored by both the Premier of New South Wales and the Japanese Consul.

There is a joining fee of A$30 to cover your one-year stay. On registering you are given a membership card with your photo on it which also acts as identification.

There are Japanese speakers present to advise you on finding share accommodation and employment. There is a weekly orientation covering all government requirements regarding working in Australia, how and where to apply for a tax file number, why it is needed, and safety. There are staff always on hand to assist with any information you may need during your stay. Japanese newspapers are there for you to read, luggage storage is available, as is a typewriter if you need to type your CV. A mail holding service is also offered.

Australia Japan Working Holiday Advisory Office
Level 5, 225 Clarence Street
Sydney NSW 2000
Tel: (02) 299 1177
Fax: (02) 299 1277

ITAS (International Travellers Advisory Services.) There is a A$25 registration fee and for this they will receive and forward your mail to anywhere in Australia and back home to you at the end of your stay.

Other services offered include one-to-one advice on finding work and arranging the first few nights' accommodation on arrival. An airport pick-up service is available (Sydney only).

Once in Sydney you can use ITAS as your office base to look for work, accommodation, etc. They have tables and chairs, cheap coffee, all the local newspapers, a pay phone facility with expert advice and guidance on the job scene.

There are noticeboards advertising jobs, share accommodation and travel information. They also offer luggage storage facilities, advice on obtaining tax file numbers, motor registration plus medical and travel insurance. There are CV/resume, word-processing and fax/photo-copy facilities you can use for a nominal fee.

ITAS is also a good meeting place for all travellers and migrants. There is a Japanese speaker on staff to assist their Japanese clientele.

ITAS
Suite 2, Level 6
38 York Street
Sydney NSW 2000
Tel: (02) 262 5011
Fax: (02) 262 5551

Traveller's Contact Point. This company will hold all your mail for you. You don't even have to go in as a quick phone call from anywhere in Australia will see your mail forwarded to you.

Traveller's Contact Point also keeps a record of where the mail is sent just in case someone is trying to find you in an emergency—say granny has kicked it. This way they have a starting point in locating you.

You can also use the address for your tax file number and for bank statements or whenever you need an address.

There is a one-off registration fee of A$35 which covers your stay in Australia of up to 12 months. If you wish to join this service from overseas, call them on 61-2-221-8744 giving your credit card details. Otherwise, pop into the office when you arrive. Mail to your contact point should be addressed as follows:

Your name
c/- Traveller's Contact Point
7th Floor, 428 George Street
Sydney NSW 2000

The Traveller's Contact Point also gives free advice on accommodation, work opportunities and travel insurance. They offer services like visa processing, luggage storage and a secretarial service if you need a CV typed. And of course, they can arrange all your travel.

Traveller's Contact Point
7th Floor, 428 George St
Sydney NSW 2000
Tel: (02) 221 8744
Fax: (02) 221 3746

Electronic voice-mail services

Australia is very big and keeping in contact can be difficult. These days though, you can keep in contact via electronic voice-mail services. These systems sounded a bit complicated when I first heard about them but they are really quite simple and it's like having your own phone number and answering machine without the initial costs.

Anyone needing to contact you, like your parents, an agency offering work, or a friend arranging a get-together, can dial the number from anywhere in the world, key in your allocated PIN and leave a message.

It is up to you then to regularly check for messages by dialling the central number and keying in your PIN for messages to be played to you. Keep a pen and paper handy to jot down contact numbers.

Teletalk Australia Pty Ltd is one of the companies providing this service. They offer a special deal whereby you receive a free 30-day membership by calling:

   +61 0552 5052   From anywhere overseas.
     0055 29440   From anywhere within Australia.

You must then enter 66 as the account number, then follow the instructions to receive your own account number and PIN.

Travelcom International offers an electronic voice-mail service plus 'Travelwatch' which is a free service. It is an optional travel safety procedure whereby you can leave a recorded security message detailing your immediate travel plans with an alert period. If you fail to update or cancel the alert by the period nominated, Travelcom will pass on relevant details to the authorities. Mum and Dad will like this service!

Other services include poste restante and mail forwarding where, if your mail is addressed to Travelcom, they will leave a message on your voice-mail. When you contact Travelcom with your location the mail is sent out to you.

Also available is 'The Card' which offers discounts, yes that wonderful word all backpackers like to hear, discounts on food, tours, travel, accommodation, etc.

They also have Classifieds where you can advertise by recording messages about employment, lift sharing, accommodation and special deals. It's also a good way to buy and/or sell vehicles, camping equipment, bikes, etc.

You can register your documents with Travelcom as well so should any be lost a copy can be retrieved. To join Travelcom contact:

Travelcom International
PO Box 2441
Cairns QLD 4870
Tel: +61 (070) 32 0387
Fax: +61 (070) 32 0756

Travel Tracker is another electronic mail service which offers a 30-day free trial on some services.

If you're setting up home in Sydney for a while you may wish to join Travel Tracker 2. This service gives you your own Sydney number. The service is proving popular with people looking for work because prospective employers think that you have your own phone number with an answer machine. Agencies don't hesitate to contact you knowing you will receive their message. It costs A$20 per month with a one-off A$5 joining fee. Contact them on:

+61 02 437 6777	From anywhere overseas
9906 6939	From within Sydney
1800 631 140.	From anywhere within Australia (except Sydney)

Useful publications and information

If you have a craving to read up on Australia then you might wish to contact the following:

The **Australian Tourist Commission** has set up Aussie Help Lines to promote Australia abroad. If you contact the Help Line numbers you can receive information on all aspects of an Australian holiday. The topics include travel tips, Aboriginal Australia, backpacking, camping, wildlife viewing, surfing, scuba diving plus much, much more.

To find Help Lines in your area, I suggest you ring the Australian

Tourist Commission on one of the following numbers :

Canada/US (Mt. Prospect)	708 296 4900
Denmark (London)	8001 8842
Finland (London)	08001 18061
France (Paris)	05 91 56 25
Germany (Frankfurt)	0130 82 51 82
Ireland (London)	44 181 780 2227
Italy (London)	1678 76043
Japan (Tokyo)	03 5214 0730
Netherlands (Frankfurt)	060 22 3428
New Zealand (Auckland)	0800 65 0303 or 09 527 1629
Norway (London)	800 11024
Sweden (London)	020 79 5267
United Kingdom (London)	0990 02 2000

The names in parentheses refer to the location where the offices are based.

Aussie Backpacker (the budget travellers' newspaper) is a bi-monthly newspaper jam-packed with up-to-date information and articles for backpackers and it includes advertisements on accommodation and travel options.

It is available free in Australia, or for A$15 *Aussie Backpacker* will send you a copy of the newspaper along with their accommodation guide before you arrive. Just ring or fax them with contact details plus your credit card number and within a week you should have some reading. If ringing, make sure you work out the time difference first. Contact them on:

Tel: +61 (077) 72 3244
Fax: +61 (077) 72 3250

TNT Magazine has long brought antipodeans living in the UK news from home and kept them up to date with travel options. Once you're in Australia you can pick up a copy of TNT's free ***For Backpackers by Backpackers*** from airports, train stations, coach terminals and most hostels. TNT Magazine also produces the ***Australia New Zealand Travel Planner*** which provides useful information for those seeking to work and holiday in Australia. Pick up your free copy at YHA Adventure Shops, All Campus Travel Shops and some Australian Embassies and High Commissions or contact:

TNT Travel Planner
14-15 Child's Place
London SW5 9RX
Tel: (44) (0171) 373 3377
Fax: (44) (0171) 373 9457

Go Australia is a publication crammed full of information for independent travellers (age open) planning a trip to Australia. It covers flight options, climate charts, travel features, guides for key cities, the culture and the wildlife.

To obtain a copy from within the UK send either a self-addressed envelope (9" x 6½") with 2 first class stamps OR a £1 cheque or postal order to the address below.

Those outside the UK should send a bank draft or money order for £2 or FOUR international reply coupons to:
GO Publishing Distribution
70 Brunswick Street
Stockton-on-Tees
Cleveland TS18 1DW
UK

Checklist

- ☐ Passport and visas in order
- ☐ Recorded passport number
- ☐ Booked air ticket
- ☐ Signed power of attorney
- ☐ Made a will
- ☐ Taken out holiday insurance
- ☐ Worked out money, opened bank account
- ☐ Arranged travellers' cheques
- ☐ Had vaccinations if needed
- ☐ Had check-up by doctor, dentist, etc.
- ☐ Have all doctor's referrals and required medication
- ☐ Pre-booked accommodation for arrival
- ☐ Pre-booked travel arrangements
- ☐ International Driver's Licence
- ☐ CMC
- ☐ Joined YHA/BRA
- ☐ Joined air mile club/s
- ☐ Obtained International Youth Card/Student card
- ☐ Joined mail holding/electronic voice-mail services
- ☐ Obtained useful publications/information—or leave until you arrive
- ☐ Updated CV and obtained all necessary references
- ☐ Backpack/suitcase packed and labelled
- ☐ Bought activity to occupy yourself on plane
- ☐ Cancelled milk and papers
- ☐ Arranged care for pets

- ☐ Left a copy of itinerary
- ☐ Remember departure tax if your country has one
- ☐ Taken a pen to fill out landing card
- ☐ Some cash for transport from airport

Travelling alone

It seems the most common reason that people sacrifice their dream of travelling in Australia is that they don't want to go alone. Yes, it is scary, and yes, you may sometimes feel uneasy, especially when you're dining in a restaurant alone, and yes, you will probably feel vulnerable, but don't let these concerns put you off. In fact, I have always found travelling with someone else a hindrance. This is because when I'm travelling with other people I tend to stay with them, but when I'm on my own I make a more concerted effort to meet other people. Still, be selective and wary of strangers. If you are worried about travelling alone, here are some tips:

- Look approachable. How? Smile at other travellers, let them know you don't mind being distracted from staring out that window or reading that book.
- Don't feel self-conscious about speaking to the person sitting next to you on the plane, train or bus, because you might just make a friend. If you do make a wally of yourself, who cares? You will probably never see them again.
- On arrival in Australia and throughout your travels stay at hostels as these are full of travellers/students, many of them on their own and looking for friends.
- Ask that room mate what they are doing for their next meal. Maybe you could catch a cheap bite together, or say you want to see a particular sight: Have you seen it? Do you want to come?
- Join in activities at the hostels, like the weekly barbecue or even watching TV—someone just might be watching their favourite show, which could be yours as well. Discuss what's happening during the ads.
- In Sydney go to ITAS or the Australian Japan Club to read the papers and noticeboards. You'll meet other travellers who have also gone there to read the papers or look at the notice boards.
- Book an organised tour like Contiki or Connections. Try the smaller tour companies too, as many single travellers take these not only to see the sights but to meet people.
- When you're travelling follow the popular backpacker routes (see the **Holidaying** section).

- If you don't have transport consider car pools.
- Sometimes employment agencies have get-togethers for their temps; go along and meet other temps.
- If you're asked to join in a social activity on work assignments, join in.
- If someone has given you the phone number of a friend of a friend of a friend, give them a call. You have nothing to lose.
- Do you know of someone at home who hasn't seen their relatives in years? Offer to pay their family a visit to pass on the latest news. They in turn might pass on tips about finding accommodation or job opportunities. They could even offer to put you up, or a free meal.
- Join a sporting team or club: cricket, soccer, basketball, netball, Rugby League, Rugby Union, AFL, tennis, sailing, etc.
- Take up an outdoor activity: learn to surf, scuba dive or sail.
- Register for an evening course, look in a library for brochures— you might want to do car maintenance if you plan on driving around Australia!
- If you don't want to eat in restaurants alone choose eateries like McDonald's and KFC where other people eat alone, or go to a food hall in a shopping centre.

So get up and go, even if it is by yourself, because you won't be by yourself for long. And you'll regret it if you don't do it.

Travelling safe

Australia is a relatively safe place to travel, though you should still take precautions to make sure you and your belongings remain safe.

As I mentioned in the 'Packing' section, try not to look like a tourist. Of course you'll want to visit the tourist spots but cameras and maps are dead giveaways. If possible try and keep cameras and maps out of sight until needed. Study the place you are going to before you get there. That way you'll look like you know where you're going and what you're doing.

Even be careful of the way you carry bags. They can easily be slit open without your knowing, particularly if they are carried slung over your back. A suggestion is to wear the bag with the bulk of it in front of you. If it is too uncomfortable to do this then ask yourself, do I need to carry all this around? If not, convert to a smaller bag. Many people carry around plastic shopping bags. Girls could wear a small shoulder bag worn with strap draped diagonally over the body with the purse in front. They'll have to take your whole body to get away with that purse.

If you decide to use a money belt don't expose it when a lot of people are around. Have your funds for the day readily available somewhere else, like a pocket. Bum bags are very popular these days—make sure they are secure and facing forward.

Do not ever leave your luggage unattended or out of sight in a public place. Two friends were once asked by another tourist for directions. As they looked at his map he moved them around so they had their backs to their bags which, of course, was a ploy so an accomplice could steal their bags. The tourist then disappeared very fast.

You should be conscious of where your valuables are at all times. Don't put wallets in your back pockets as they can easily be snatched. If a commotion breaks out around you hold your valuables close to you and move away as quickly as possible.

It is strongly advised not to leave valuables in hostel rooms. It is sad to say, but sometimes it's other travellers you need to be wary of. Most hostels have safes where you could leave things.

When counting your money do it in private. If there isn't any privacy in your hostel, find the loo (toilet) and sit there for a while.

When getting to know your travel companions, don't disclose your financial situation or where you hide that credit card.

In long-term accommodation you might want to put a lock on your bedroom door or on the wardrobe.

Girls: even though Australians like to dress casually, don't be too casual or provocative. Too-short shorts and revealing t-shirts will bring out the primitive instincts in men, sometimes inviting unwanted advances and/or insults. It can also bring out the green-eyed monster in other females who can do nasty things.

Other tips:
- At work keep your belongings close to you.
- Don't go into parks and gardens after dark.
- Let someone know your itinerary and keep in contact. If you say you will contact them, do so. Otherwise they might get worried.
- **Do not hitchhike.**
- Walk in the middle of the footpath, away from the kerb, to avoid drive-by snatchers.
- At ATMs be careful of muggers—be aware of anyone behind you.
- When you're travelling by car, try not to leave your valuables in a place where they can be easily seen.
- If you don't trust the door to your accommodation, put something against it which will make a noise when moved.

Travelling well

Time only will tell if you travel well or not. Hopefully most of us have grown out of travel sickness but for those who suffer there are preparations available, so see your chemist, doctor or health food shop. Prevention is the best method.

If you've never flown before or just feel anxious about it, avoid drinking stimulants such as coffee, tea and alcohol. Drink calming camomile tea or take a non-addictive herbal relaxant such as valerian. If your ears pop during landing and take-off swallowing helps, along with sucking a lolly (sweet).

Even though it is preferred that you stay in your seat during a flight, get up and move around occasionally. Sitting for long periods of time inhibits circulation. Simple exercises done in your seat will help:

Starting with your feet, rotate your ankles in both directions then stretch and wiggle your toes. Press your knees together and tighten your buttocks. Pull in your stomach. Rotate your wrists. Stretch and shake your fingers out. Rotate your shoulders; raise them up and down then backwards and forwards. Slowly rotate your neck. Have a big stretch. You can do these on long bus and train journeys also, along with any other exercise you invent or discover.

Sleeping, between contortions, is the hardest thing to do on a plane, bus, train or car. You might want to invest in an inflatable pillow to support your neck. Maybe a prescribed sleeping tablet will help you.

Jetlag is every traveller's nightmare. I read that it is worse if you travel east to west, or was that west to east? Whichever way you go, jetlag seems pretty unavoidable. I was told in a health food shop that studies have shown people with high zinc levels recover more quickly from jetlag. A supplement before, during and after the flight might help. Or else on arrival you can go out, get drunk and blame it on the hangover which you know you'll recover from.

Request only light meals for the flight and drink plenty of water so you don't dehydrate. Spend a little time on the plane pampering yourself by cleaning your teeth, brushing your hair, washing your face and applying liberal amounts of moisturiser. All these things will make you feel fresher.

When you reach your destination try not to sleep until the evening, so you get your body used to the new time. Easier said than done, I know. Go for a walk or to the gym or the beach or pool if your hotel has them, to take some exercise. Take a long re-hydrating bath or shower and apply plenty of moisturiser. You may want to put tea bags on your eyes to reduce any puffiness. Try inverted posture to cure swollen ankles.

Some people take a stop-over, which is a good idea as it breaks the long flight. If you can't sleep on planes you might prefer to try a day-flight if it's possible. Then you can sleep at night when you get off.

Even the best cast-iron stomachs can react to foreign foods. The only thing to do is eat new things in moderation, drink fizzy drinks (non-alcoholic) if you're feeling queasy and take some Quick-Eze or antacid.

Girls taking oral contraception should watch out for the time difference. There is plenty of sanitary wear available, though in remote areas it is a little scarce and can be quite expensive, so take supplies.

Some girls take oral contraceptives continuously to avoid having their periods while travelling. This is something to consider.

A bout of diarrhoea or vomiting only a few hours after taking a pill can mean it has not been absorbed into your system so, once again, take precautions.

3 Arriving in Australia

Arriving on a sea vessel

For those who arrive by ocean liner or freighter, customs officials will board the vessel to conduct procedures before allowing you to disembark.

If you're arriving on a small vessel the captain must first call a **Proclaimed Port of Entry** (various ports along the coastline) a few hours before arrival so customs, quarantine, and immigration formalities can be put into motion.

Arriving on a plane from a foreign country

As I mentioned before, the gateways to Australia are Sydney, Melbourne, Brisbane, Perth, Adelaide, Darwin and Cairns with Sydney being the most popular and busiest.

All travellers entering Australia, including Australians returning home, must fill in a **Travellers' Statement** and an **Incoming Passenger Card**.

The Travellers' Statement asks questions relating to customs and quarantine, like: are you bringing any plants, animals, illegal substances, etc. into the country? Have you exceeded duty-free allowances? You should be honest in case you are searched.

The Incoming Passenger Card asks for your vital details such as name, passport number, date of birth, etc.

These forms are handed out by airline staff on the plane a few hours prior to your arrival. Sometimes your travel agent will give them to you.

When the plane has completely stopped you are required to remain on the plane to be sprayed. Officials from the **Australian Quarantine**

Service board the plane, line you up along the aisles and with your arms in the air and your legs apart, spray your every nook and cranny to kill any germs you might have brought with you. No, no, I'm just kidding about this! But officials from Australian Quarantine do board the plane. While you are still seated, they or the airline staff walk down the aisle releasing a spray from aerosol cans which eliminates any nasties on the plane. So if the person next to you shrivels up and disappears with a squeal and a pop don't worry about it. No, no, just kidding again. It is harmless to humans, though for a couple of seconds it can be a little unpleasant. You might want to look down and/or maybe cover your nose and mouth. It's not that we don't trust you but we are very strict about what is brought into the country and this ultimately benefits us all.

Once you're off the plane, follow the signs or everybody else to the **Entry Control Point** where you will hand over your travellers' statement, incoming passenger card and passport to a customs official.

Have at hand any proof the official might require, like travellers' cheques or a return ticket. They don't usually check these items but be prepared in case they do.

If asked about your visit, remember that you are on a holiday first and only hope to find casual work to further your travels around the country.

Along with your passport you will be given back your travellers' statement form which you should keep handy.

Next, **collect your luggage** from the carousels—hopefully you won't have too long to wait.

After picking up your luggage, head either to the **green channel** if you have no goods to declare, or the **red channel** if you do have goods to declare. You will hand over your travellers' statement to a customs official at the beginning of the channels, who will instruct you to proceed through or send you to an area for your goods to be checked.

Once through, welcome to Oz.

Arriving at Sydney airport

Sydney's Kingsford-Smith International Airport is named after Sir Charles Kingsford-Smith, who forged his way into our history books by pioneering long distance air travel. Just think, if he hadn't had such an interest in flying, visitors might still be arriving in Sydney after a month-long voyage at sea.

The airport is situated at Mascot (locals often refer to it as Mascot airport) with the runways built into Botany Bay.

There are two terminals, the international and the domestic, so make sure you go to the right one for future flights. They are linked by bus if you make a blunder.

For those arriving on an international flight, you will of course arrive at the international terminal. Because the airport is built in the Sydney Metropolitan Area it has a curfew and is open from 6 am to 11 pm. Most international flights are timed to arrive in the morning and leave in the afternoon. If several flights land at the airport in the morning (which is usually the case), and yours is one of them, be prepared for a wait to get through the procedures.

There are two levels to the terminal; arrivals are downstairs and departures upstairs. Before you leave the international terminal you might wish to visit the information centre and pick up all the accommodation and sightseeing brochures, free backpacker magazines and papers that you can carry. If you haven't booked any accommodation enquire as to what is available.

If you want a place to sit and gather your thoughts, or to read through all the accumulated paraphernalia you've collected there is plenty of seating downstairs, but you might wish to go upstairs where there is a food hall. There is also a bookstore with a range of travel guides if you didn't purchase one before you left home.

If you don't have anyone to greet you or a pre-arranged lift, you will want to get to your accommodation as soon as possible.

Transport from Sydney airport

Taxis are plentiful outside the terminal on the arrival level, with taxi drivers happy to take you to the front door of your accommodation. Don't be deterred if the driver looks in the street directory, or gives it to you to give him directions; unlike other countries, taxi drivers in Australia do not need to know where every street is.

A taxi fare varies with how far you are travelling, and during week days you might find yourself in peak hour traffic. Before you hop in you can always ask the driver to advise a rough estimate of the journey price then decide whether to go or not.

A trip into the city costs around A$20. If there are a few of you sharing a taxi the cost is quite reasonable.

The green and gold **Airport Express** bus can get you to the city. There are two routes: Route 300 which takes you into the city and Route 350 which travels to Kings Cross. At the time of publication the cost is A$5 for a one-way trip on either of the two routes and the buses run every 20–30 minutes.

There is an outside kiosk on the arrival level of the airport where you can buy your ticket, and the guys behind the counter usually don't mind answering a question or two if you're unsure about getting to where you're going. If you can, pick up a brochure which lists the stops, including many of the major hotels and backpacker hostels.

You could buy a three, five or seven-day **Sydney Pass** instead of just a ride on the Airport Express as this tourist ticket covers a return trip on the Airport Express, travel on the Sydney Red Explorer bus (see the **Holidaying** section), the blue Bondi and Bay Explorer bus (see the **Holidaying** section), regular Sydney buses and ferries (see the **Holidaying** section), ferry cruises, JetCats and RiverCats. It would definitely help you get around the city, not only to see the sights but to help you get settled.

At the time of publication, a three-day pass costs A$60, a five-day pass A$80 and a seven-day pass A$90.

Also servicing the airport is the **Sydney Airporter** that takes passengers to hotels in the city, Kings Cross and Darling Harbour. Some public buses also stop at the airport. Their terminals are outside the arrival level.

Cars can be rented at the airport. Request a map and directions to your destination.

Arriving at the other international airports

The procedures for arriving at the other international air terminals around Australia are the same as those for Sydney.

You will have your forms to fill in, be sprayed after landing and go through the same immigration and customs procedures.

All the airports are serviced by transport. Each one has an airport bus that will take you into the city and the drivers are happy to drop you off at your accommodation or near it. There are also taxis and car rental companies.

Accommodation noticeboards are usually on hand near information centres.

4 Now you've arrived

There are a few formalities which are necessary. I strongly suggest you spend a day doing these to get them out of the way.

Pick up a **map** of the city you're in so you can find your way around! Your accommodation might have a free one, or go to an information centre.

If you're settling into long-term accommodation you may wish to obtain a **street directory** which has a more extensive listing of streets. These can be bought from newsagents, bookshops and some petrol stations.

When you know where you're going (well, sort of), the next thing on your agenda is to claim your account or **open a bank account** if you haven't already done so from home.

Unlike residents of Australia who must follow the 100-point identification system to open an account, non-residents (working holidaymakers) only need to provide a passport as identification. You will also need an address so paying the fees for contact addresses with ITAS, Traveller's Contact Point or the Australia Japan Office will prove worthwhile.

The major banks with many branches spread throughout Australia are ANZ, the Commonwealth Bank, the National Australia Bank and Westpac. It's your choice which one you open an account with as the various services are all quite competitive, but many opt for the Commonwealth as post offices all over the country will make simple deposits and withdrawals for you if you have trouble finding a Commonwealth branch. There are other banks and building societies as well so shop around.

Most people open an interest-bearing savings account with an ATM card attached so they can operate the account at ATMs and through EFTPOS facilities.

These accounts require you to keep a minimum of A$500 in the account otherwise charges will be incurred. The annoying thing about banking in Australia is the State and Federal taxes on transactions. The banks will provide you with details of these.

Each bank calls their ATM cards and machines by different names. ANZ has the Day & Night card for the Day & Night bank, the Commonwealth has the Autocard for the Autobank, the National Australia has the Flexicard for the Flexiteller and Westpac has the Handycard for the Handybank. These machines are joining forces so a card from one bank can be used in another bank's machine; for example National Australia cards can be used in ANZ machines and State Bank machines.

While you're travelling, it is much easier to posses an ATM card as you can get money out whenever you need it. ATMs are open 24 hours a day and though they are sometimes closed due to a mechanical/computer failure, they are usually very reliable.

Apply for a **tax file number**. This number is extremely important to your existence in Australia as all workers MUST have one. If you don't, 47% of your salary will be taken in tax instead of 29%. So it is worth your while to get this number unless you plan to work illegally!

You will need an application form to apply for this number and these are available from any tax office. Applications can be mailed in but this means that original documents (ie. your passport) must be sent with the application in order to prove your identity. The number can take about 28 days to come through therefore I suggest that you go into a tax office and apply in person so you can keep your documents. You may need them to register for work or open a bank account. If you don't mind being separated from your documents then go ahead and send them because they are returned to you by registered post—but do you have an address yet?

Take your passport and International Driver's Licence for proof of identification to one of the main offices listed below.

Sydney:	100 Market Street
Melbourne:	2 Lonsdale Street
Brisbane:	140 Creek Street
Perth:	45 Francis Street
Adelaide:	191 Pulteney Street
Hobart:	200 Collins Street
Darwin:	Cnr Mitchell and Briggs Streets

When you begin a new job you'll need to advise your employer of your tax file number so they can tax you correctly. If you don't have one they usually give you a few weeks' grace to supply them with it. If you don't, you will be taxed accordingly.

Those from the UK, New Zealand, Sweden, the Netherlands, Finland, Malta and Italy might wish to register for a **Medicare** card. There is a brochure available at Medicare offices if you wish to read more about the reciprocal medical arrangements. It isn't necessary to register but you never know if/when you'll get sick so it might be best to register in case it's ever needed.

In regard to payment it would be easier to be registered as many doctors bulk bill, which means you hand over your Medicare card, it is run through a card reader, then the doctor claims the payment direct from Medicare. If they don't bulk bill you will have to pay the fee then claim a rebate from Medicare.

Contact mail holding services and electronic mail to pick up mail and messages.

If you hope to find **long-term accommodation** (see the **Accommodation** section) it would be wise to begin looking before you start work as, once you're at work you might not be able to use a phone for contacting possible abodes. If you do find a place you may also need someone around to let in the personnel connecting gas, electricity and phone services.

Other things to do include picking up free copies of backpacker magazines.

Where to start in Sydney

The main areas in Sydney for working holidaymakers to start are the areas where the hostels are concentrated. Hostels are a great source of information. In Sydney they are found in Glebe, Manly, Coogee, Bondi and the place that everyone is told to avoid yet which still manages to be the most popular haunt, Kings Cross. Remember—if you don't like an area you can always leave.

Kings Cross: Along the main drag and in the side streets there is cheap accommodation available. 'The Cross'—as it is affectionately called—comes alive at night so the further away from the main street you can find accommodation the quieter it will be. There are quite a few hostels along Victoria Street which is the one behind the main street. The airport express bus has drop-off points along Victoria Street.

Kings Cross is also serviced by public buses and has a train station linking it to the city. A ten-minute walk will find you in the city centre.

There are two exits from the train station; the east side which takes you to Victoria Street and the west side which takes you to the main street, Darlinghurst Road.

Along the main street there are banks, coffee shops, restaurants, souvenir shops, real estate agents, night clubs, newsagents, tattoo shops, prostitutes, laundromats, travel agents, car rentals, the Traveller's Autobarn, the Backpackers' Car Market, etc. Everything you need.

Glebe: This area is also a popular starting place as the two YHA hostels are there. It is easily reached by airport express and public buses. It's easy to get to the city also.

Manly: A seaside suburb on the north side of Sydney Harbour, Manly is a little trickier to get to from the airport as you need to catch the bus to Circular Quay and then catch a ferry across the harbour.

It is well serviced for those working in either North Sydney or the city and offers everything the backpacker needs. It is a half-hour ferry ride to get to the city, which is a novelty at first, but many find that it is too out-of-the-way.

Bondi: You'll find this a very popular place, especially with the Kiwis, visiting Brits and the Irish. There are two parts to Bondi, the Junction and the Beach. The trains end at Bondi Junction and to get to the beach you will need to catch a bus.

Once you have the formalities under control you can get on with what you came for—having a good time!

5 Accommodation

Accommodation is diverse in Australia and ranges from tents, campervans, hostels, farm stays, homesteads, units and town houses to terraces, three bedroom brick homes, budget hotel chains and five star hotels. Quite a wide choice really!

As a working holidaymaker you will spend a lot of time travelling and therefore need short-term accommodation. This is readily available in Australia. If staying put for a while, you will want something more permanent, such as a flat or a house share, which can be a little harder to find.

Short-term accommodation

Glossy accommodation brochures only scratch the surface of the lodgings available to you and mostly cater to those prepared to pay a day's salary for the privilege. As a working holidaymaker you will only stay in such places for a little luxury. Most travellers stay in hostels. In Australia there are YHA hostels and independently owned hostels with many belonging to the BRA (Backpacker Resorts of Australia) chain.

Hostels

Most hostels have a minibus offering a courtesy lift from the bus/train/airport. When they know you are arriving they will be there to meet you. Some allow you to call at any time for a lift to the hostel.

Almost all the hostels include free sheets, pillow cases and blankets in the nightly price or they can be rented at a minimal cost, which will save you having to carry around your own sheet and sleeping bag.

Airconditioning is something to consider, especially in the Northern Territory and Far North Queensland.

Twenty-four-hour access is also important as you don't want or need curfews—remember you left mum and dad at home. Most hostels don't have a curfew.

Other things to look out for include: help finding work; personal lockers in rooms; fully equipped clean kitchen with enough room in fridge/s to leave food; TV/common room; laundry with a soap machine and iron; phones; travel booking service; luggage storage facilities; safety deposit boxes; fans if airconditioning isn't available in hot weather and heating in cold weather; apple pie and ice cream; free tea and coffee; breakfast; party nights; barbecues; swimming pool; bathrooms that are cleaned daily; en-suite toilets and showers; an information lounge; discounts for seven-day stays; elevator to all floors; prime site e.g. near the beach.

So, with all that is on offer how do you choose a hostel to stay in? Fellow travellers are a great source of advice on hostels, they can either recommend or pan one. After all, isn't that what a fellow traveller is for? To pass on useful information!

You really do need to have an idea of what you want from a hostel; do you want a party hostel or a quiet one? If you read their advertisements you can usually tell. For instance a small, quiet, family-run hostel should give you a good night's sleep and have a communal area if you want to socialise. Some hostels advertise their backpacker party nights, so of course those that do should be party hostels. Choose what you want.

Accommodation in hostels is dormitory-style, with varying numbers of beds (bunks) in a room. The number of occupants per room can vary from 4 up to 12 or more. Some dorms are single sex while others can be mixed dorms. You should know what you prefer when booking or checking in. Some hostel owners (not many but there are some) have only $$$ signs in their eyes and if you don't request a bed in, say an all-male 4-bed dorm, they could put you in an 8-bed mixed dorm.

Some hostels are now offering single, double and twin rooms but be prepared to pay extra to stay in them and note, they are limited.

Dorm living is an experience if you aren't used to it. You will be sharing with people you've never met before, but you should have a common goal—to travel Australia.

Be prepared for people changing in front of you, having little or no privacy, people coming in late and getting up early, zippers zipping, bags rustling, alarms going off, snorers, talkers and even bonkers, who are usually embarrassed in the morning.

Even though you want to travel as cheaply as possible, I have met people whose health has been affected. A male friend always seemed to have snorers in his dorm and he was becoming crankier and crankier as the days passed from lack of sleep. If this happens to you then paying a few bucks more at a cheap hotel for a good night's sleep would be worth it.

Security in hostels

Sometimes it's not professional thieves you have to worry about, but your fellow travellers. Be careful in hostels with your personal belongings, especially your valuables. There are transients who steal things like jewellery or cameras and sell them quickly—in places like Kings Cross there are quite a few hock shops. As I've said before, don't keep all your valuables together, or if you do, keep them with you at all times. You should even take them to the shower with you in one of those handy plastic bags I recommended you bring so they won't get wet.

When unpacking or packing your bag try and do it when no one else is around—I know that can be hard to do.

Be careful with all your things because other popular items to go missing include that expensive shampoo and conditioner you've just specially bought to bring life back to your hair, or that new deodorant, or that carton of milk, or that new t-shirt—some cheap travellers don't have any regard for other travellers' items and it's sad to say, but that's how they survive.

Staying healthy in hostels

As I mentioned before, sleep deprivation is a health hazard. So are bad eating habits.

Hostels usually have a communal kitchen for you to use. Many feel self-conscious about cooking and eating in front of others who aren't. If this is you, maybe your room mates might want to share a cooked meal with you. Easy things to cook include pasta dishes—a bag of pasta and a bottle of sauce can be easily bought at supermarkets and are relatively cheap. So is soup and a bread roll.

I know that when you're on your own it can be easy to pop into McDonald's, KFC or a pizza place for a bite to eat, but do try and eat healthily.

YHA are renowned around the world for offering affordable accommodation and Australian YHA hostels are no different. They are situated in all the major tourist areas you are likely to visit and include many services. The hostels can be classified as simple, standard or superior. As well as clean, budget accommodation, they offer 24-hour access, laundry facilities, TV rooms, communal lounges and communal kitchens or bistros. One thing I liked about some of the hostels was the light above my bed. By using this light, early risers and late night revellers do not need to disturb everyone else.

When you join the YHA, obtain their accommodation guide so you can plan your travels.

BRA and independently-owned hostels

As an increasing number of independent travellers are choosing to visit Australia, the demand for budget accommodation is growing. To survive in this competitive market hostels have improved dramatically and not only are they offering clean, comfortable and affordable accommodation, but many other things as well to entice you to stay with them. Some hostels participate in the Backpackers Classification Scheme in which they are classified by backpacks instead of stars. The more backpacks, the better the hostel. The scheme is voluntary and not all hostels have been classified, so they do vary in quality. Use your discretion. Ask to see the room first before you pay, or only pay for one night so that, if you don't like it, you can leave.

Hostel services being offered include a 1800 number which is toll-free, so you can phone the hostel from anywhere in Australia and they pay for the call. This is very useful if you don't have small change and saves you the expense of ringing ahead to book a bed, which can be costly.

Sydney hostels

As well as the hostels in Kings Cross and Glebe there are many hostels in beach areas like Coogee and Manly.

Kings Cross is the mecca for privately owned backpacker hostels. Most of them are old and shabby but people still stay there. It is about a 10-minute walk into the city and is serviced by buses and trains. The main drag has many eateries and at night the place comes alive. Some of the pubs have backpacker nights. There is a concentration of hostels on Victoria Street (the Airport Express stops outside) and more are scattered along the main road and side streets.

Glebe is another popular area backpackers choose—the two Sydney YHA hostels are here. It is an inner city suburb that has become popular in recent years, with many yuppies and trendies or whatever you want to call them moving into the terrace houses. It has plenty of cheap eateries, a good night life and is well serviced by public transport to the city.

Coogee is a popular beach area in the Eastern suburbs of Sydney. As well as being close to the beach, the area has all the amenities you need. It is well serviced by State Transit buses for getting into the city.

Manly is a popular beach area north of the city. The ferries run regularly between the city and Manly, and you'll also find an abundance of services for travellers in the seaside suburb.

YHA, BRA and independent hostels range in price from around A$12–16 per person per night for a bed in a dorm and a few dollars more for a twin, double or single room. Some hostels have weekly rates and don't mind you staying longer while others believe that hostels are for travellers only and have a limit on how long you are allowed to stay.

How to find hostels
Carry a copy of the YHA or BRA accommodation guides for easy reference. *Aussie Backpacker* magazine and STA Travel both have free accommodation booklets. Also look in the backpacker magazines where the hostels advertise.

The airports have accommodation boards where you can choose a place to stay. There is usually a free-phone service available which connects you directly to the accommodation advertised, or the people behind the information counters can advise you. Hostels often have a representative meeting planes, trains and buses to offer accommodation.

Camping/caravan parks
There are many places to camp around Australia, with many camp sites ideally located near beaches or in bushland surroundings.

Facilities vary from caravan park to caravan park. The facilities on offer can include a swimming pool, tennis court, laundry, shop or mini-mart, games room and clean amenities blocks.

If you don't have your own tent or campervan you can still stay at camping grounds and caravan parks, as they often have permanent tents, on-site vans, cabins and villas which can sleep 6–8 people. Permanent tents are on powered sites so you will be able to cook and possibly watch TV—what a luxury.

B&B (Bed and Breakfast)
These are more a novelty in Australia and are a little pricey for the average backpacker, but you might like a weekend treat, or some luxury on arrival before you find somewhere more permanent. For more information, you can contact the address below:
B&B Australia
PO Box 408
Gordon NSW 2072

Farm stays
Options like this are available to those wanting to relax on a working farm. Accommodation can be in the farmer's homestead or in private quarters.
If you want to experience such a stay, information centres in each state have listings of participating farms.

Pubs and hotels

In country areas accommodation can be found in **pubs**. The quality can vary but the novelty is the attraction. Be careful of Friday and Saturday nights as a band might be playing or a disco raging and it might affect accommodation upstairs. If the pub is on a main road, watch out for traffic noise.

There are also **hotel chains** like the Budget Hotel Chain, Best Western, Golden Chain and Flag Inns, which you can stay at. A little costly for single travellers but still an option.

Long-term accommodation

It's an Aussie dream to own a home. It's a backpacker's dream just to find somewhere to unpack the backpack!

If you're one of the lucky ones who has a bed or even a floor to sleep on, you're off to a good start; finding rental accommodation for only a few months can be a daunting task.

There are hostels that allow long-term stays but if you can make a commitment for a few months, moving into a flat or house is the way to go.

Renting a flat/house

Renting a flat or house does require a commitment of at least three months but it seems that nobody really wants the responsibility of having their name on a lease, so if you are travelling alone moving into an established flat or house is ideal. This way you only need to worry about paying the weekly rent and any expenses.

There is a lot of competition for decent rooms in flat and house shares, as many travellers want to get out of a hostel and spread out, which is only natural. You do have the choice of either living with other travellers or sharing with an Australian. A greater commitment is required if you're living with an Australian as they will prefer someone staying long-term. But hey, people move in and out of flats all the time, just look at the classifieds. If you are asked how long you intend staying you can always say indefinitely, then if you decide to go travelling after a couple of months that is totally up to you.

Moving into a travellers' flat can be more relaxed as they are used to people going off travelling. When you move in, sort out how the bills are paid; do you buy your own food or is there a kitty which everyone contributes to? Particular times for the bathroom; a roster for chores, etc. Many travellers may be frugal and with no formal commitment to bind them can easily pack up and take off leaving bills behind.

Beware of freeloaders also. During your travels you will meet up with a lot of people and many won't say no to a free night's accommodation on your floor. Sometimes a night can increase to a few days then a week, etc. They should make some kind of contribution.

Sometimes sharing a flat or house can lead to a communal existence. If you've heard stories of ten people living in a three-bedroom flat, believe it; these rumours are true as many travellers want cheap accommodation, and this is one way to do it. You will need to be an easy-going person to live like this because you won't have much privacy, but the social life should be great.

A room in a flat or house share can be around A$100 a week. With two of you in a room this works out cheaper.

Setting up a flat or house

If there is a group of you, you could set up your own flat. First you have to find one and when you do, most landlords require 4 to 8 weeks' rent in advance plus a bond. So if you find, say, a two-bedroom place at A$200 a week, it could cost up to A$2400 just to move in.

If you have never rented before there is a renting guide available from real estate agents which explains the rights and responsibilities of tenants and landlords.

All bonds (deposits) paid in Australia must be registered with the Bond Board which is a government-run board overseeing bond monies. Real estate agents can register your bond for you. The Bond Board holds and invests the money, so on its return you may receive some interest.

When you move out, an inspection of the flat or house is undertaken. If there is no damage, etc. the board is notified and you will receive your bond back, usually within a few days. Payment can be made in various ways such as a cash cheque or direct credit to an account.

Be careful of hidden extras such as fees or bonds for connecting the phone (which you will need if looking for work), electricity and gas.

At the time of publication a phone connection cost $A216 and a re-connection A$50. When you're looking a place over, check whether a phone line has already been connected so you only have to re-connect it.

If you plan to make interstate phone calls a deposit of A$250 is required. If you want to make overseas calls a deposit of A$500 is required. If you have the latter facility make sure you keep a record of phone calls, though they will be itemised on the bill, as some travellers have been known to make calls and then disappear. A suggestion could be to have overseas calls as incoming only.

There will be a monthly rental fee on the phone line and the equipment.

You will need to have the electricity connected. If it is already connected have it changed to your name because you don't want to have to pay for the previous tenant's bills.

At the time of publication a security bond of A$120 is required to connect electricity. Have it connected during office hours, as on weekends and after hours it costs an extra A$40.

When you leave, the deposit can go towards your final bill. To receive any money owing a cheque will be sent so if you have moved out, the mail holding services of ITAS, Traveller's Contact Point or Australia Japan Working Holiday Advisory Service will come in handy.

If your residence has natural gas, it might already be connected; it isn't usually disconnected. Just make sure to change over the name when you move in. As with electricity, you don't want the previous tenant's bill to pay.

At the time of publication a security deposit of A$100 is required plus A$20 to establish an account with AGL (Australian Gas). The security deposit can go towards paying the final bill. You can also get it back by cheque or through one of the showrooms as long as it has been authorised by the accounts section first.

For connection of the above services look in the phone book for their correct numbers.

Leaving before lease is up

If you want out of your lease before the time is up you will have to pay money for the time that the flat or house will be unoccupied. If you can find someone to take over the lease for the remaining time, such as another traveller, you can usually roll over the lease and bond. Check with your landlord, agent and the rent board about this.

Finding a flat or house share

Hostel noticeboards often advertise vacancies in flats. Look in the Saturday and local papers or visit a real estate agent.

Most rentals are for six months though you will find shorter leases for three months. Most properties are unfurnished but furnished properties can be found. They will cost more but will suit you better as you don't want to buy furniture. You could rent some though.

When visiting real estate agents dress neatly, as that first impression counts. If they don't like the look of you because you've come from the beach to see them, they can tell you nothing is available.

I know you can't hide your accent, but don't mention you are a backpacker on a working holiday as their attitude can change. I have found this especially so in Kings Cross. They often think: Another backpacker, you're a risk, and don't have the time of day for you.

So don't let them treat you like a second-class citizen. Play them at their own game and dress appropriately—maybe in your work clothes which will show them you are employed. Produce references. They do prefer them to be Australian but if overseas ones are all you have, then so be it. Try to commit for as long as possible.

An option I have found while researching this guide is **holiday flats/units** to rent which will be fully furnished, usually serviced, studios or 1, 2 and 3-bedroom places.

These work out to be more expensive than taking a flat through a lease (possibly twice as much, even more during school holidays) but hey, you won't have a bond to pay, you won't have to connect and pay for electricity, gas and phone or have the worry of fulfilling that six-month commitment. Holiday flats can be rented weekly or monthly which means you have more control over your time. It's an option to think about.

Look in the yellow pages under accommodation, holiday or serviced apartments to find places.

Also consider **guest houses** which offer accommodation. Look in the yellow pages for them.

Another option is companies offering a **match-up service**. Someone looking for a place pays a registration fee to the company to match them up with someone with a room or place to rent. There is no guarantee this will prove fruitful and in most cases people with places to rent prefer people who can make a commitment. It's another option to think about.

Living in Sydney

Many working holidaymakers set up home in Sydney. Accommodation ranges from blocks of flats and units to inner city terraces to 3-bedroom fibro and brick homes.

The Sydney metropolitan area can be divided into roughly five areas: the inner city suburbs, the eastern suburbs, the northern suburbs, the southern suburbs and the western suburbs.

Most travellers find accommodation in the inner city suburbs around Glebe, Surry Hills and Newtown. Other popular places are Woolloomooloo, Elizabeth Bay, Bondi and Coogee which are in the eastern suburbs. Living near a beach is a favourite option, as you can come home from a hard day's work and go for a swim or surf. These areas are also close to the city for work opportunities.

The northern suburbs are often referred to as the 'silvertail suburbs' because the rich and famous favour the north shore of the harbour. Working holidaymakers once again favour the beach suburbs, notably Manly, but many young Australians live near and around North Sydney as it is close to work, the public transport is good and there are loads of eateries and pubs to try.

The western suburbs are a little far out for working holidaymakers as are most southern suburbs, though there are some beautiful beaches and long-term accommodation places available.

Living in other parts of Australia

To find long-term accommodation in other areas of Australia look in the local papers, possibly stay at caravan parks and contact real estate agents.

Possessions insurance

Though you should be travelling light, shouldn't need to purchase furniture and should be covered by holiday insurance, you might want to insure your personal effects if you move into a more permanent abode. Contact the insurance companies to insure your belongings.

6 Work opportunities

There are many work opportunities in Australia for the traveller seeking casual employment, which is good news. Even better news is that I and other travellers have all found work relatively easy to come by. Having a variety of skills, being prepared to try new things even without the appropriate skills and having the desire to get out and find work, all enhance one's prospects.

Employers have told me that the two things that let working holidaymakers down in their quest for finding work is lack of commitment and reliability. Yes, you are here to enjoy yourself, which employers are well aware of, but if you find work you will be expected to work for the period you commit yourself to. Many just work until they get some funds and then take off. This has unfortunately meant that in some professions, job-hunting travellers have a bad reputation. For instance, some who find work on a prawn trawler think it is a holiday on a boat in the sun. Not so, and many captains don't like taking on travellers now for this reason. So please: if you take on a position, try and fulfil your commitment as future working holidaymakers are depending on you to keep work opportunities available.

In this chapter I've tried to include as many work opportunities as possible. Of course not every profession can be covered as some of them are too specific, require qualifications to be recognised, or involve sitting for tests—all too time-consuming and costly for a working holidaymaker, but hey, this gives you the perfect excuse to try something completely different like fruit and vegetable picking, cooking on a prawn trawler, working as a jackaroo or jillaroo, serving in a roadhouse or working on an island resort—positions which will truly give you a taste of the Australian way of life.

You shouldn't expect to be on the same level as you are at home; after all, the work is meant to be casual. Most work is found in the capital cities, namely Sydney, but there are opportunities all over the country.

When you go looking for work one of the things that lets you down is not having a contact number. Did you organise an electronic mail service? In Sydney you can use ITAS as your office base to look for work—see 'Mail Holding/Advisory Services' in **Organise yourself before you go** for the details.

Working and studying

For those who are nearing the end of their one-year working holiday visa and are looking for a legal way to stay, or for those who are too old to qualify for the working holiday visa, you might consider looking into the **student visa**. You need to undertake a full-time corse in order to qualify, but you are allowed to work during this time.

Australia is fast becoming the place chosen by overseas students to learn English and further their education. This decision is influenced by favourable weather, the opportunity to travel, being able to work while studying and the high standard of qualifications obtained.

There are certain conditions you must adhere to: depart Australia on the expiry of your student visa; satisfy your course requirements and have valid enrolment; you are permitted to take 20 hours of casual work per week; maintain adequate health insurance.

For those wishing to learn English there are English Language Intensive Courses for Overseas Students (ELICOS) courses available.

All schools are of a high standard and need accreditation. Contact ELICOS for a brochure which covers course details and schools:

ELICOS
43 Murray Street
Pyrmont NSW 2009
Australia
Tel: +61 02 660 6455
Fax: +61 02 566 2230

Furthering education
Overseas students are most likely to be furthering their education. So, what's available? Further education is available through TAFE (Technical and Further Education) colleges and through universities. So how do you choose where to study?

Magabook Pty Ltd is a Sydney-based company which produces three very useful publications for those wishing to study in Australia.
- *Study and Travel in Australia*
- *A Guide to Australian Universities*
- *Studies in Australia* (for those from Canada and USA)

These guides give an overview of the Australian education system plus offering general advice and providing useful information to aid future students. There are also school, college and university listings. These publications are available free, though there is a small postage charge. Contact:

Magabook Pty Ltd
PO Box 552
Randwick
Sydney NSW 2031
Tel: +61 02 398 2555
Fax: +61 02 399 9465

Working in Sydney and the rest of NSW

Many travellers set up home for 3–9 months and work in Sydney. There are a variety of employment opportunities available for the working holidaymaker, including both indoor and outdoor work.

Work can be found all over the Sydney Metropolitan area. Most office work is found in the Central Business District that runs from Circular Quay to Central. North Sydney is also a popular office-based work area. There is another business centre at Parramatta in the western suburbs. You will find many agencies have offices in the city, North Sydney and Parramatta.

The industrial areas are found in the south and south-west of the city. Building work is available in various areas in the city and the suburbs.

There are pockets of work for office dwellers and industrialists down south in Wollongong and up north in Newcastle where the steel works are.

Work as fruit and vegetable pickers can be obtained in various New South Wales areas.

Hospitality work can be found all over the state but mostly in favourite beach holiday areas along the coast, and in the ski resorts during winter.

Working in other States

Queensland is known as the Holiday State, and there is a lot of hospitality work available along the coast, especially in areas such as the Gold Coast and Cairns and on island resorts.

Office-based work could be found in Brisbane and other major centres such as Townsville.

Outback Queensland stations might need farm hands, and fishing trawlers may want deck hands. There is plenty of fruit and vegetable picking work available, especially around Bundaberg, Childers and Innisfail for most of the year.

Most people prefer to holiday rather than work in the **Northern Territory** as towns are remote with long distances between them.

Work can be found in the Territory on outback stations and in the resorts at Ayers Rock/Uluru and Kakadu. There is fruit and vegetable picking in two areas—Kununurra and Katherine. There are a few office support agencies in Darwin where you might obtain some work.

Most of **South Australia** is desert so there is not much work there, but in Adelaide you may pick up some office support, hospitality or industrial work.

Fruit and vegetable picking is also available in the wine growing areas of the Barossa Valley. Just think, in a few years' time when you uncork a bottle of Australian wine you can think back to those days when you carefully cut branches of grapes from their vines.

Tasmania is often forgotten on the working holiday itinerary. The most available work is fruit and vegetable picking, and possibly some office work in Hobart or Launceston.

Victoria is an industrial state with agricultural work in many areas.

Melbourne offers various types of employment for office workers, and hospitality work can be found in Lygon and Brunswick Streets which are renowned for their restaurants.

Hospitality work could also be found in the Victorian ski resorts during winter

Western Australia is a big state and much of it is desert. Perth does offer office and hospitality opportunities though.

There is a little agricultural work, and also work on stations in the Kimberley region.

Hospitality work can be found in the popular Northbridge area of Perth and along the southern coastline.

Finding work

The various ways to find work include through the CES (Commonwealth Employment Service), through temporary agencies, hostels, word of mouth and door knocking.

Work through the CES

The CES (Commonwealth Employment Service) is government-run and its aim is to find work for Australia's unemployed. So how can the CES help a working holidaymaker looking for casual work? Well, I have heard reports varying from 'Yes they found me a few days' work' to 'They didn't/couldn't do anything for me'. It does depend on which office you try and at what time of year you try it. For instance a suburban CES might not be able to help you, whereas a CES in an agricultural area which is just coming into harvest season might greet you with open arms.

You can go into any CES office in cities and towns throughout Australia and look at the job boards without having to register. They are categorised, for example into clerical, trades, sales, casual and part-time, etc. If you feel they can help you then you will need to register.

You don't really have to be dressed up but there is a minimum dress code of shorts, a t-shirt and footwear. Make sure you bring your passport, proof of your working visa and your tax file number with you. Oh, and a pen just in case the government ones have liberated themselves for a better life.

In the major cities there are City Casuals and/or Templines. Positions through City Casuals are mostly manual, which means you need to be fairly strong and fit. The work could be unloading containers at the docks, moving furniture, or as factory hands or kitchen and counter hands.

In Sydney, City Casuals is at 10 Quay Street, Ultimo. You must be there by 7.00 am, leave your name on a list and remain there until 10.00 am (take a book to read and a coffee to keep you awake if you are not used to early mornings), at which time if you haven't been offered work you usually go home but will be kept on the list. You might have to go back for a few days before work is offered.

Work is offered to people who have been on the list the longest, so get there early. You also need to be able to do the job.

Work is for a minimum of three hours which can sometimes stretch to a day or even longer. You can be requested back by employers on other occasions.

Working holidaymakers in Sydney can also try the Haymarket CES, 699 George Street, Broadway where, due to the amount of enquiries from backpackers, a special backpackers' section has been set up. You can also check out the temporary boards while you're there. Make sure you take your working holiday visa and tax file number with you.

Those of you with office skills might want to register with Templine which places people in temporary office support positions, mostly in the government sector.

Work through temporary agencies

Temporary agencies were originally the way women re-entered the work force; thus the abundance of office support agencies. Employers these days have realised the potential and flexibility gained from employing experienced staff through temping, outsourcing and contracting so now there are agencies covering a whole gamut of skilled and unskilled professions.

Unlike agencies in some countries which are situated on roadsides and don't mind you walking in off the street, Australian agencies are tucked away in high-rise buildings. Even if a consultant is readily available most will want you to make an appointment.

When you attend your appointment make sure you dress appropriately. I have waited in many agency receptions and seen consultants look prospective temps up and down. It is their belief that if you don't dress properly for them (after all, they are your employer), you will not dress properly for their much-valued clients. For office-based work, dressing appropriately means a corporate wardrobe. For other professions such as a chef you don't have to wear your uniform, just dress neatly.

Besides dressing appropriately you should take with you an updated curriculum vitae (CV) which should state your name, contact details, age, schooling, qualifications and list your employment history from the most recent position to the earliest. You should also have a couple of references that can be confirmed. Yes, agencies will contact your country of origin if they feel it necessary. You should also be prepared to have your skills tested, e.g. a typing test or a literacy test which can take a couple of hours.

Take your passport, as employers like to see your working visa. They'll also want your tax file number so they can deduct the correct tax when you begin work, and your bank details to credit your salary.

When registering, ask about the rate you can expect to receive. Rates are usually determined by what skills you will be using on the assignment, though some agencies put you on a specific hourly rate.

Agencies are not allowed to charge you a fee for finding you work as they charge the client. If any do want a fee they may be breaking the law. The laws can vary though and I have discovered that Victorian nursing agencies at present can and do charge you a fee.

Be honest and tell agencies what your skills are so that they can place you in an appropriate position. Don't let an agency bully you into accepting a position you know you can't do. Some agencies will do this just to fill the position, although most have in-house training programmes to make you more marketable.

Agencies expect you to be flexible and to adapt to their clients' needs. If you find yourself in a situation you don't like, don't just get up and leave. Once I was assigned to a place where I really couldn't stand the boss so I rang the agency. We arranged for me to go home sick while the agency found someone new to fill the position. The agency never held this against me.

Try not to get involved in the politics of the place. Be courteous, punctual and appropriately dressed. A good rule of thumb is to dress up the first day, see what everyone else is wearing then blend in the next day. Do not abuse the telephones.

Note that many agencies send out appraisal forms for feedback on your performance. This, in turn, can lead to your being requested again.

As I mentioned, there are temporary agencies specialising in a broad spectrum of work opportunities, and I have tried to give details of as many as possible. There is no guarantee that you will obtain work through them, but to give yourself the best possible chance you should register with more than one agency.

It is usually best to register early in the week, as from mid-week to the week-end salaries are paid and consultants are busy. On Thursdays and Fridays agencies ring their clients to find out their temp requirements for the following week.

To keep your consultant up-to-date with your availability, try and ring in at least once a day, preferably early in the morning so that if a job comes in you are fresh in their minds.

When agencies are offering you an assignment they will go through some details with you first. They should tell you the nature of the position, the skills required, some background information on the company, the full address and how to get there if you don't know. They should advise on any dress code, how long the assignment is for and most importantly the rate you will be receiving. Once you've accepted the assignment they will send you a time sheet. If you don't have one because the assignment is only for the day, ask the client to list on their letterhead how many hours worked, the date worked and your name, and have them sign it.

Payment from agencies is weekly (on receipt of your signed time sheet), on a certain day determined by them.

I've also tried to give details of agencies with offices in various other cities as well as Sydney, so your details can be sent on if you wish to work in another place. Agencies with only one office shouldn't be overlooked however, as sometimes you can get lost in the crowd working through the bigger agencies.

Some of the agencies have many offices in one city. For instance in Sydney, there are various suburban branches of the larger consultancies. I have included only the central city office address of the agencies here, as most working holidaymakers will probably find accommodation close to the city due to their lack of transport. You can always ask the agency or look in the phone book to find the location of the other offices, which are mostly in North Sydney or Parramatta.

Where possible I've noted agencies with offices outside Australia so you can contact them and have your details sent over. But remember—all agencies will need to meet you here in Australia before placing you in work. Australian officials can be a little suspicious of your motives if you pre-arrange work; remember, the working holiday visa is mainly for you to have a holiday and find incidental work to supplement your funds. But having contacts is no crime.

The agencies listed are in alphabetical order and not in order of my preference. I have chosen them as they are happy to take on travellers. They are just a sample of the agencies available.

Any included rates of pay are just a rough guide and were the latest at the time of publication. They can change though, so you shouldn't automatically expect to receive them.

Australia is going through the process of changing to eight digit telephone and fax numbers, so if you have problems with any of the phone or fax numbers listed below, contact directory enquiries.

When writing from overseas, remember to include 'Australia' in the address. See the section on 'post' in **Useful Information**.

Work through hostels

Hostels can be a great source of work.

They are mostly staffed by travellers so you could be working on reception, cleaning or driving the courtesy minibus to pick up other travellers from the airport or bus station. This work is usually found by being in the right place at the right time. So become friendly with the staff already there and make it known that you are looking for work.

Hostel noticeboards are very good sources of job information as many local employers contact the hostels when they require staff. Employers who need staff quickly often approach hostels, as they know there will be travellers there eager for a day's work no matter what it is.

Hostels in agricultural areas such as Bowen and Bundaberg are always looking for backpackers to work.

Advertisements on noticeboards I've seen include: cricket umpire, swimming pool attendant, lawn mower, security guard, serving beers at the races, serving pies at the Easter Show, setting up tents and manning stalls in a circus, food preparation on a crocodile farm, telemarketing, singing telegrams, leaflet drops, handyman, courier, Santa Claus, house removalist, jackaroo/jillaroo.

Other places to look for work include the local and major papers. The best days for the major papers are Saturday and Wednesday. For nursing work it is Thursday, and for computer work look in the Tuesday edition of *The Australian*.

Door knocking is another way to find work especially waitressing, bar work and labouring.

Many travellers aren't aware that tourist brochures can give you an idea of what work is available in a particular area. Some examples are:

Industrial centre—trade positions.
Mining town—trade positions, hospitality.
The town servicing the farming community—agricultural positions.
Holiday resorts—hospitality.
Major regional centre—office support, accounting, hospitality.

So when you find a place you like and you wish to stay a while, find out about the local industry.

Fellow travellers are also a good source of advice on work prospects, so don't be afraid to let it be known you are looking for work. A simple question like 'Do you know of any work going?' just might prove fruitful.

What's taken from your salary?

That beautiful thing, tax, is always taken from your salary. You must have a tax file number in order to be taxed correctly. Employers usually give you a month's leeway to supply them with one, after which time you will be taxed at a higher rate if you've failed to advise them of it.

The percentage taken out for travellers (non-residents) is on a scale with 4 levels.

If your weekly wage is between A$0–A$397, 29% tax is taken out. For example, if you earned A$300 for the week, 29% of A$300 is A$87, so you would receive A$213 in your pocket.

If your weekly wage is between A$398–A$729, A$115.13 (which is 29% of A$397) plus 34 cents for each A$1 over A$397 is taken out. So if you earned A$600 for the week, the first $A397 is taxed at 29% (A$115.13) and the remaining A$203 is taxed at 34% (A$69.02); therefore, from your A$600, A$184.15 is taken, leaving you with a take-home pay of A$415.85. Confused yet?

The third level is for weekly earnings between A$730–A$960, where you will be taxed A$228.01 plus 43 cents for every dollar over A$729.

The 4th level is for weekly earnings of A$961 and over, where A$327.27 plus 47 cents for every dollar over A$960 is taken.

If you want to know more about tax for non-residents ask your payroll officer or contact the tax department.

Some professions might require you to join a trade union and the fees for this are taken out of your salary. This is usually just a couple of dollars a week.

It became compulsory in the late 1980s for every worker to have a superannuation fund. 'Super', as we call it, isn't taken from your salary but an amount equal to 4% is paid by your employer into a superannuation fund on your behalf. For casual workers you must earn over A$450 a month for this to be paid. When you leave your employer, make sure you ask if you are entitled to your fund. It is meant to be rolled over from employer to employer until you retire but if it is less than A$500 it is usually paid to you in cash.

If you need clarification of deductions from your salary speak to your payroll officer.

Make sure when you leave an employer you obtain a Group Certificate for tax purposes.

Accounting

Accounting work covers a range of positions including data entry operators, account clerks, bookkeepers, part-qualified accountants, qualified accountants and auditors. These positions can be found in commercial, financial and industrial sectors throughout Australia, though for the traveller your best bet is to look in the capital cities, with the concentration of work along the east coast, namely Sydney, Melbourne and Brisbane.

Overseas qualifications of CIMA, ACCA, ACA and AAT are recognised by agencies and you do not need to register with a governing body unless you are planning to practice full-time.

The more qualifications and experience you have the greater number of positions available to you. These days it's preferred that you have spreadsheet experience. Lotus and Excel are very popular, so if you can gain knowledge of these it will increase your marketability not only here but also when you go home. If you're not familiar with these popular spreadsheet programs but you do have experience on other software packages, agencies will often cross-train you, which means they can place you in more positions benefiting not only you, but themselves and their clients.

Rates of pay vary depending on your experience and the job you are placed in. Therefore a data entry operator or accounts clerk could earn A$13–14.50 an hour while a bookkeeper could expect A$15–17, an assistant accountant A$18–19 and a fully qualified financial accountant A$20 and over. Remember, rates of pay depend on the individual agency and the skills you will be performing in the position where you are placed.

Length of assignments can vary from a few days to weeks or longer but, to keep within working visa restrictions, usually no more than three months.

Work is fairly constant throughout the year, though May to August are usually busy as 30 June marks the end of Australia's financial year. Before this date companies are preparing annual accounts, and afterwards they need to balance and report. Many firms do have a company year end that falls at a different date to the official financial year end and they often need help during that time. Another busy time is around November/December when many are tying up loose ends to go on summer holidays.

Accounting positions are advertised in the newspapers or can be found through agencies who specialise in the field. Contact one of the following:

Accountancy Link aids many working holidaymakers in finding temporary work. They are affiliated with Harrison Willis in the UK who can provide you with a letter of referral.

Sydney office	**Melbourne office**
Level 3, 2 Bligh Street	Level 16, 600 Bourke Street
Sydney NSW 2000	Melbourne VIC 3000
Tel: (02) 233 1077	Tel: (03) 9670 6251
Fax: (02) 223 1050	Fax: (03) 9670 3402

Accountancy Placements have offices all over Australia and take on many travellers. They are associated with Accountancy Personnel in the UK who can send your details to Australia for you.

Sydney	**Adelaide**	(08) 8231 0820
Level 11, Chifley Tower	**Brisbane**	(07) 3839 5011
2 Chifley Square	**Canberra**	(06) 257 6344
Sydney NSW 2000	**Melbourne**	(03) 9614 2443
Tel: (02) 232 6266	**Perth**	(09) 322 5198
Fax: (02) 221 4287		

Accountants on Call

Sydney	**Brisbane**	(07) 3221 1855
Level 11, 45 Clarence Street	**Melbourne**	(03) 9621 3399
Sydney NSW 2000		
Tel: (02) 290 2399		
Fax: (02) 290 2020		

Bligh Appointments is an Australian-owned company established in London in 1974 which employs many working holidaymakers commuting between Sydney and London.

Sydney office
9th floor, Dymocks Building
428 George Street
Sydney NSW 2000
Tel: (02) 235 3699   Fax: (02) 221 3480
Before you leave for Australia, any additional information you require may be obtained from:
London office
131–135 Earls Court Road
London SW5 9RH
Tel: (0171) 244 7277 Fax: (0171) 835 1251

Michael Page Finance places many travellers in accounting positions. They can also place candidates in banking and financial positions.
Sydney office   **Melbourne** (03) 9600 1633
Level 19, 1 York Street
Sydney NSW 2000
Tel: (02) 235 1488   Fax: (02) 251 1444

Michael Page also has offices in The Netherlands (Amsterdam, Eindhoven), Germany (Dusseldorf, Frankfurt) and the UK through which your details can be forwarded to Australia.

Michael Page Group PLC has a travel pack to aid you with your trip to Australia. Enquire at:
London office
Page House, 39/41 Parker Street
London WC2B 5lH
Tel: (0171) 831 2000 Fax: (0171) 831 6662

Temporary Solutions place many travellers in accounting and office support (see the 'Office Support' section) positions.
Sydney   **Brisbane** (07) 3221 1677
Level 12, 275 George Street   **Melbourne** (03) 9621 2288
Sydney NSW 2000
Tel: (02) 377 9677   Fax: (02) 377 9688

Western Staff Services have 400 offices worldwide.
Sydney   **Adelaide** (08) 8212 4202
Level 8, 20 Barrack Street   **Brisbane** (07) 3221 8949
Sydney NSW 2000   **Canberra** (06) 249 7777
Tel: (02) 299 5400   **Darwin**   (089) 815 365
Fax: (02) 299 2525   **Melbourne** (03) 9696 5500
                                          Perth   (09) 321 4104

Agriculture

It is possible to work your way around the country picking fruit and vegetables. If you look at the maps following (courtesy of Mark Taylor) you will see where picking work is available and when.

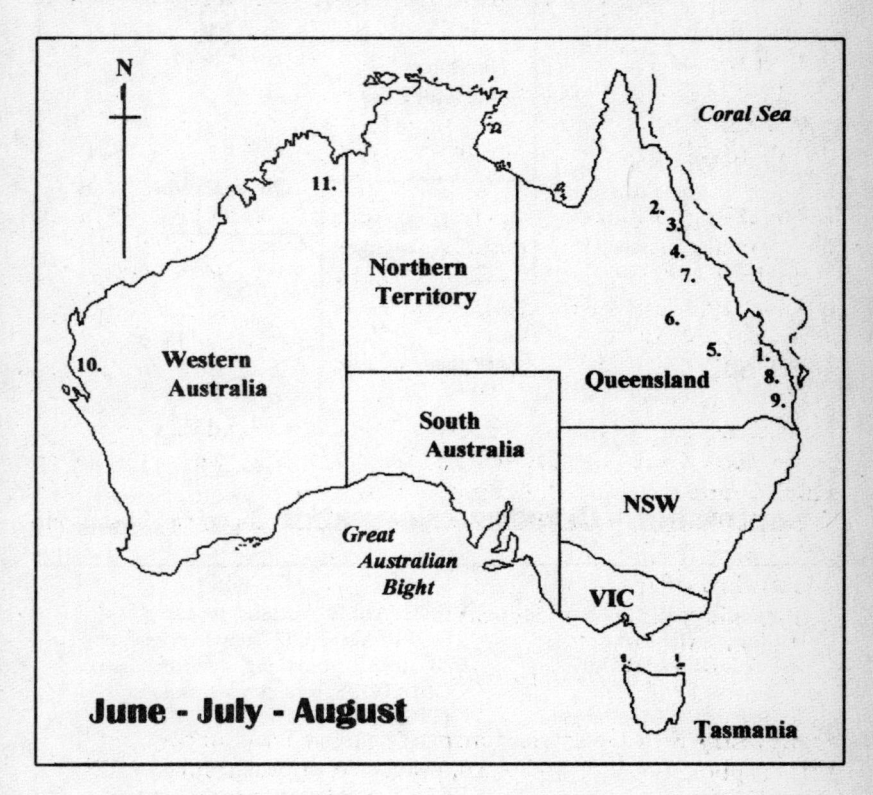

June - July - August

1. Bundaberg & Childers — VEGETABLES, melons, avocados
2. Atherton Tableland — TROPICAL FRUIT, strawberries
3. Tully, Cardwell & Innisfail — BANANAS, pumpkins, watermelons
4. Bowen — TOMATOES, capsicums, mangoes
5. Gayndah & Mundubbera — CITRUS FRUIT
6. Emerald — CITRUS FRUIT
7. Ayr — TOMATOES, capsicums, mangoes
8. Gympie — BEANS, other vegetables
9. Sunshine Coast & Nambour — STRAWBERRIES, zucchinis
10. Carnarvon — TOMATOES, capsicums, bananas
11. Kununurra — MELONS, vegetables, bananas

September - October - November

1. Bundaberg & Childers — VEGETABLES, melons, avocados
2. Atherton Tableland — TROPICAL FRUIT, strawberries
3. Tully, Cardwell & Innisfail — BANANAS, pumpkins, watermelons
4. Bowen — TOMATOES, capsicums, mangoes
5. Gayndah & Mundubbera — CITRUS FRUIT
6. Emerald — CITRUS FRUIT
7. Ayr — TOMATOES, capsicums, mangoes
8. Gympie — BEANS, other vegetables
9. Dimbulah — TOBACCO
10. Stanthorpe — VEGETABLES, apples
11. Kununurra — MELONS, vegetables, bananas
12. Katherine — MANGOES
13. Carnarvon — TOMATOES, capsicums, bananas
14. Young — CHERRIES
15. Cowra — ASPARAGUS

Work opportunities

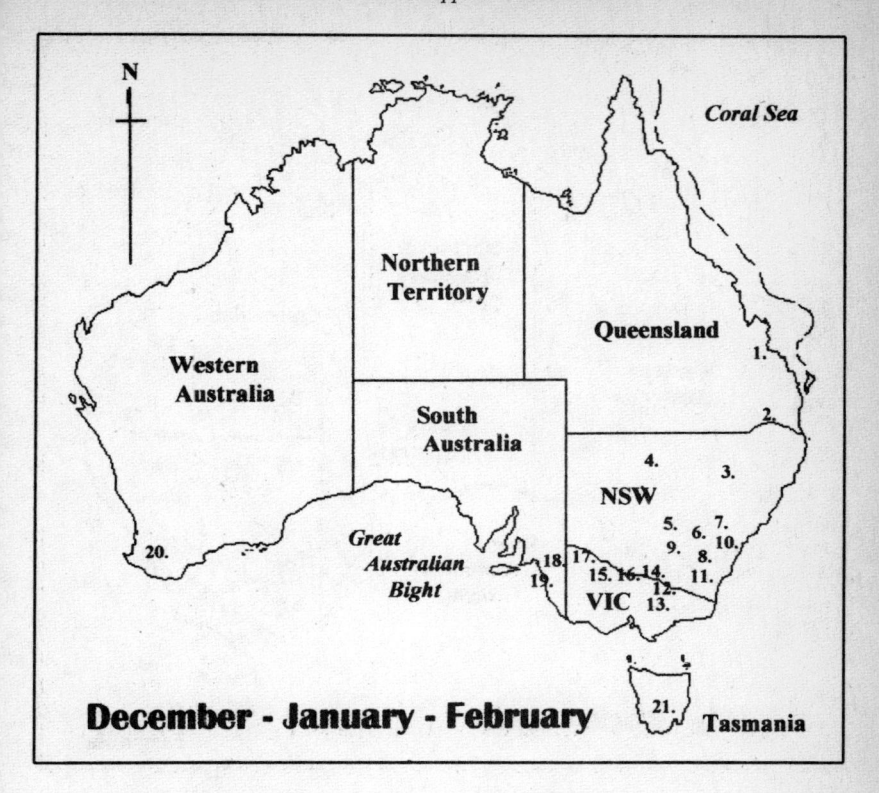

December - January - February

1. Bundaberg & Childers — VEGETABLES, melons, avocados
2. Stanthorpe — VEGETABLES, apples
3. Moree — COTTON CHIPPING
4. Bourke — ROCKMELONS
5. Forbes — VEGETABLES, apples, grapes
6. Orange — APPLES, cherries
7. Bathurst — STONE FRUIT
8. Young — CHERRIES
9. Griffith & Leeton — GRAPES, citrus, onions
10. Bilpin — APPLES
11. Batlow — APPLES
12. Cobram — PEARS, peaches, apples
13. Shepparton — PEARS, peaches, apples
14. Barham — CITRUS
15. Robinvale — GRAPES
16. Nyah — GRAPES
17. Mildura — GRAPES, citrus
18. Riverland — GRAPES, citrus
19. Adelaide Hills — APPLES
20. Donnybrook — APPLES, vegetables
21. Huon Valley — APPLES, cherries

March - April - May

1. Bundaberg & Childers — VEGETABLES, melons, avocados
2. Stanthorpe — VEGETABLES, apples
3. Tully — BANANAS, pumpkins, watermelons
4. Gayndah-Mundubbera — CITRUS FRUIT
5. Forbes — VEGETABLES, apples, grapes
6. Orange — APPLES, cherries
7. Griffith & Leeton — GRAPES, citrus, onions
8. Batlow — APPLES
9. Cobram — PEARS, peaches, apples
10. Shepparton — PEARS, peaches, apples
11. Mildura — GRAPES, citrus
12. Robinvale — GRAPES
13. Nyah — GRAPES
14. Riverland — GRAPES, citrus
15. Adelaide Hills — APPLES
16. Barossa Valley — GRAPES
17. Clare Valley — GRAPES
18. Donnybrook — APPLES, vegetables
19. Huon Valley — APPLES, cherries
20. Tamar Valley & Scottsdale — APPLES, hops

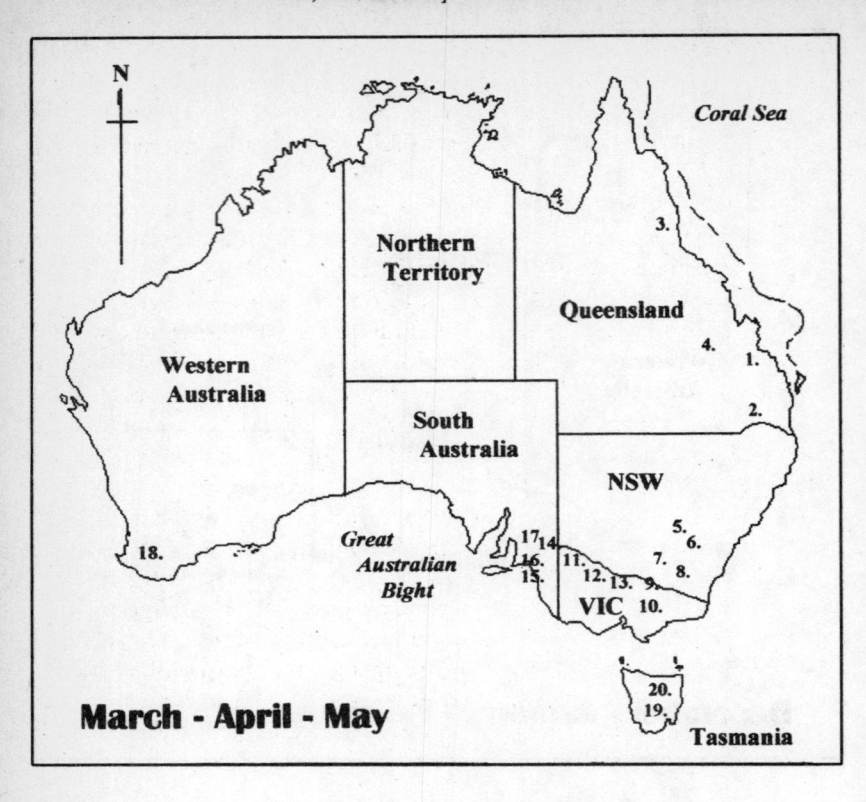

What to expect

If you have never done this type of work before you might like to consider which crop you'd prefer to pick. For instance, would you prefer climbing a ladder in fruit tree orchards or bending over picking ground crops?

Many of us hate early morning starts but with fruit and vegetable picking they are a necessity. You will find that if the day is going to be a scorcher you are better off starting early in the morning anyway.

Before you begin work you should find out from the grower the hours you are required to work, including the starting time and any house rules. If you decide you don't like the work after a few days, can you leave and be paid when you leave? Some growers only pay every fortnight and require a fortnight's notice to quit. Most importantly, find out how much you will be paid so you and the grower know where you both stand.

Payment is calculated either by an hourly rate, which depends on the crop, or by the bin load. Your grower will advise you.

Your own transport isn't essential to get to the harvesting areas as most are accessible by public transport, or a lift can be arranged.

Accommodation isn't always provided, though some orchards have simple huts and an area to camp. Some of the larger orchards, especially in Northern Victoria, provide meals for a nominal fee or have kitchens available for use. If no accommodation is available backpacker hostels and caravan parks are usually located in the area. Check all this out before you head off.

As the work is outdoors you will encounter various elements, some of them harsh. You should have a wide-brimmed hat to keep the sun off your face. A cap is more practical for working in trees. Wear suntan lotion or preferably cover up with long sleeves and pants—the lighter and older your clothes are the better. Make sure you take a water bottle with you, as not all growers will supply you with a cold drink and you don't want to dehydrate. Take insect repellent to keep away flies and mozzies.

For cold weather conditions it is advisable to take thermal underwear as jumpers and coats can be cumbersome. A pair of fingerless gloves might also be useful. A raincoat or waterproof jacket will be handy in wet weather though work usually stops when it rains.

You should have your own pair of sturdy gloves—there are special ones with dimpled palms for citrus picking—and good sturdy shoes, preferably boots and spats or gaiters.

Check if you need to bring any equipment such as a small knife with a curved edge for grape picking, a pair of secateurs or your own buckets. Hopefully the grower will have spare ones.

Most work can be found through the local CES and the hostels in the various areas, or contact the growers themselves. It is wise to ring before you arrive as the ripening time for crops can vary from those shown on the maps, due to erratic rainfall, unseasonal cold weather, drought, etc. You don't want to turn up and find that you have a couple of weeks to wait before you begin work.

You might wish to obtain a copy of *A Traveller's Guide to the Australian Fruit and Vegetable Harvest* by Mark Taylor. A seasoned picker himself, he describes in detail the fruit and vegetable areas, includes specific regional maps locating available accommodation and indicates where to find the CES, bus terminals, train stations and orchards. He also provides contact details, information on how to get to each area plus what to do in your spare time and his book offers extremely useful tips such as the best way to place your ladder for easier picking, which can only add to your earning potential.

Copies can be obtained by sending a cheque or money order for A$10 (includes postage and packaging) inside Australia and A$15 (includes postage and packaging) outside Australia to:

Mark Taylor
PO Box 420
Gymea NSW 2227

He also has a regular newsletter called *From the Grapevine* to keep you up-to-date on what's happening in the fruit and vegetable picking world.

A year's subscription for 4 issues—spring, summer, autumn and winter—is A$5 (includes postage and packaging).

If you'd like to experience life working on an organic farm you could **WWOOF** your way around the country. No, no, you don't have to do dog impressions, even though you will find yourself digging in the dirt. WWOOF stands for Willing Workers on Organic Farms and is an exchange program.

In exchange for your willingness to work, you'll receive food, somewhere to sleep, first-hand knowledge of agricultural methods and experience your host's way of life.

In Australia there are nearly 500 participating farms; some 50 in Tasmania, 20 in South Australia, 65 in Victoria, 150 in New South Wales, 95 in Queensland, 2 in the Northern Territory and 40 in Western Australia. They are listed in a booklet available from the organisation listed below.

The full range of vegetable, fruit, dairy, pasture and arable farms are covered. They range from self-sufficient holdings through to fully commercial operations. Your duties on the farms will therefore vary depending on where you decide to work. It is accepted that 4–6 hours work per day is the average.

Bookings from overseas should be made by mail, but once you're in Australia it is acceptable to contact host families by phone.

The minimum length of stay is two nights with an average stay lasting about six or seven days, though you can arrange longer stays with your host.

WWOOF membership is per person or per couple and includes your Aussie Farm List and basic insurance to cover you while you're working on the farms. It costs A$25 per single or A$30 per couple and can be sent via an international bank draft to:

WWOOFers (Willing Workers on Organic Farms)
Mt. Murrindal Co-operative
Buchan Victoria 3885
Tel: (051) 550 218

Au pair work

In some countries the main reason for being an au pair is to learn the local language. Not so in Australia, though some do think the Australian vernacular is another language!

No formal qualifications or experience are required to be an au pair, but a liking for children and a willingness to help with household tasks like running errands, shopping, walking the dog and doing housework is essential.

Positions are live-in where you will have your own room, be provided with meals and receive a small wage. Most families like someone available for 3–6 months but shorter assignments are available which will fit in nicely with the requirements of the working holiday visa.

On average your family will prefer you to work for 25–30 hours per week, for which you will receive a salary of around A$120. Longer hours may be required, for which you will be paid extra. Sort out your hours, duties and wages before you take the position.

To find au pair work, thumb through the employment section of major Saturday papers or local papers. There are also agencies which can assist:

Au pair Australia is a licensed agency located near Sydney, which arranges au pairs for families in Sydney, sometimes other capitals, major cities, and country areas.

You may contact Au Pair Australia before arriving in Australia, but an administration fee is charged for being met on arrival and for your application form to be sent to suitable families.

Alternatively, contact the agency after you arrive when no fee is charged to arrange interviews with families. Contact Mrs Genelle Thomson who runs Au pair Australia at:

Au Pair Australia
6 Wilford Street
Corrimal NSW 2518
Tel: +61 (042) 846412
Fax: +61 (042) 854896

The Au paire Connection
This licensed company was established in 1984. It is based in Sydney but also covers positions in the country regions and major cities along the east coast. You can contact them before you arrive:

The Au paire Connection
PO Box 686
Balgowlah NSW 2093
Tel: (02) 9971 0102
Fax: (02) 9971 5579
Mobile: 018 169 875
Balgowlah is a Sydney suburb

Alternatively, you can contact Priority Placements in the UK who can forward your details to them.

Priority Placements
2 Place Farm
Wheathampstead Hertfordshire AL4 8SB
Tel: (015) 82 834 112
Fax: (015) 82 834 113

There are other au pair agencies which advertise in the backpacker magazines if the above can't help you.

Banking, finance and stockbroking

Positions are available in banking, finance and stockbroking.

Banking positions include: Business analysts, foreign exchange, fund managers and administrators, customer service, etc.

Finance positions include: Lending officers (consumer and commercial); acceptance, collections and leasing officers; credit analysts, etc.

Stockbroking positions include: private client, institutional and corporate advisers.

Work is mostly in the major cities. Specialist financial qualifications are not fully recognised in Australia and conversion courses may be required, so travellers should be flexible about the positions they accept. Do not expect to do the same job as you do at home or at the same level.

Corporate dress is required. For positions in these fields look in the newspapers or contact one of the following:

Banking Placements is a specialist recruitment consultancy for the banking and finance industry, recruiting experienced people at all levels in the key areas of money markets, foreign exchange, futures, options, equities, funds management, superannuation and investment, merchant and retail banking.

Sydney
Level 11, Chifley Tower
2 Chifley Square
Sydney NSW 2000
Tel: (02) 232 6266
Fax: (02) 221 4347

Melbourne (03) 9614 2443

Gilt Edge Appointments Pty Ltd specialise in placing permanent and temporary staff in the banking and finance industries. Positions include scrip clerks, FX/MM settlements clerks, lending/securities, account–investment, systems analysts and new issues clerks. They will accept CVs from overseas before you arrive.

Sydney
Level 10, 191 Clarence Street
Sydney NSW 2000
Tel: (02) 262 1366
Fax: (02) 262 4792

Michael Page Finance place many travellers in banking and financial positions. See their details under the 'Accounting' section.

Bars

Bar work is available in pubs, night clubs, RSL clubs, trade union clubs, sporting clubs, hotels, holiday resorts, etc. Knowing how to mix cocktails will increase your potential for finding work.

Bar work is usually found by knocking on doors, though there are agencies which can find you work. See the section under 'Hospitality and Resort Work'.

Buskers

Busking can be done pretty much anywhere, though the most popular places to ply your trade include shopping malls, outside or near tourist attractions, and public transport stations.

Profitable times are during the lunchtime rush and before or after business hours when people are either on their way to work or going home. You could try busking outside popular attractions on a Sunday when many families go out for the day. The Christmas season is always the best time and people often make extra money around then.

As there are a lot of buskers, those who try something different like mime artists or didgeridoo players often draw more crowds than those singing with a guitar.

You might contact various resorts and pubs in holiday areas for gigs.

Charity collecting

Worthwhile charities always require willing travellers to collect funds for them.

The Australian Quadraplegic Association assists people with severe physical disabilities in developing new skills which will enable them to actively participate in a variety of everyday activities. In this way, the disabled are helped towards maximum independence. As a charity collector you will help the association carry out its vital work, and be paid for it.

Australian Quadraplegic Association
Suite 204, 2nd Floor
64-76 Kippax Street
Surry Hills NSW 2010
Tel: (02) 281 8214

The Wilderness Society was formed in 1977 after it successfully prevented the damming of the famous Franklin River in Tasmania. Since then the society's continuing aim has been the protection, promotion and preservation of natural wilderness areas.

The Wilderness Society raises awareness and funds through fundraisers wearing furry koala suits. If you want to keep biodiversity alive and well for future generations, become a koala and get paid for it too.

The Wilderness Society
1st Floor, 263 Broadway
Glebe NSW 2037
Tel: (02) 552 2355

Child/elder carers

Positions for child/elder carers are available to those with knowledge of caring either through qualifications or experience. So if you have a background in nannying, geriatric nursing, social work, occupational therapy, etc. this knowledge will stand you in good stead for this kind of work.

Due to the three-month restriction on working for one employer the length of bookings can vary from 1 to 30 days, but may be extended in 30 day periods. Duties will be discussed with you before you take the position.

If you are available to live-in you are more likely to be given work. A driver's licence is also useful. Live-out positions are available but you may need your own vehicle; if you are placed as an elder carer you may need to transport your client for therapies and medical appointments, etc. If you are driving a car with children aboard, make sure they are properly restrained in their seats. The correct seat should be in the car, but as children are always growing make sure the seat is comfortable, i.e. not too tight.

For live-in, short-term positions you can expect to receive in excess of A$90 per day plus accommodation and meals. Short-term live-out positions are usually paid an hourly rate of A$12.

To find positions look in the Saturday papers or contact an agency such as **Dial-an-Angel**, which has offices all over Australia and is pleased to place travellers in child/elder carer positions. Their offices are listed following. Contact them on arrival or before you arrive by sending your CV and references. It is preferable to have a contact fax number as faxes can be sent at any time.

NSW OFFICES

Lindfield
Suite 1, 'The Colonnade'
2 Kohia Lane
Lindfield NSW 2070
Tel: (02) 416 7511
Fax: (02) 416 9400

Edgecliff
Suites 20 and 21, 'Edgecliff Mews'
201 New South Head Road
Edgecliff NSW 2027
Tel: (02) 362 4225
Fax: (02) 362 4001

Lindfield and Edgecliff are both suburbs in Sydney.

Newcastle
Suite 1, 71–73 King Street
Newcastle NSW 2300
Tel: (049) 293 065
Fax: (049) 291 551

Penrith and the Blue Mountains
Tel: (047) 22 33 55
Mobile: 019 926 215
Newcastle is 2 hours north of Sydney while Penrith and the Blue Mountains are 2 hours west.

QUEENSLAND OFFICES
Indooroopilly
Suite 3,
21 Station Road
Indooroopilly QLD 4068
Tel: (07) 3878 1077
Fax: (07) 3878 2730

Southport
Ground Floor,
33 Scarborough Street
Southport QLD 4215
Tel: (07) 55 91 88 91
Fax: (07) 55 91 86 99

Indooroopilly is a suburb of Brisbane, while Southport is on the Gold Coast.

VICTORIAN OFFICE
Balaclava
Suite 14, 285 Carlisle Street
Balaclava VIC 3181
Tel: (03) 9525 9261
Fax: (03) 9527 8680
Balaclava is a suburb of Melbourne.

SOUTH AUSTRALIA OFFICE
North Adelaide
Suite 7, 88 Melbourne Street
North Adelaide SA 5006
Tel: (08) 8267 3700
Fax: (08) 8267 3733

WESTERN AUSTRALIA OFFICE
North Perth
Floor 1, 362 Fitzgerald Street
North Perth WA 6006
Tel: (09) 328 3336
Fax: (09) 328 3710

Computer contracting

Positions range from technical support, network support and help desk support, to analyst/programmers and project managers working on mainframes, mini computers or personal computers.

Positions are on a contract basis and vary in length.

Most computer work is found in the capital cities, especially Sydney; to a lesser extent Brisbane, Melbourne and Canberra. It is possible to find this kind of work in Perth and Adelaide as well, but positions are few.

To find such employment look in the Tuesday edition of *The Australian*, in the Saturday papers, or contact one of the following agencies:

ADIA Information Technology Resources
Sydney   **Melbourne** (03) 9621 1244
280 George Street
Sydney NSW 2000
Tel: (02) 233 6577   Fax: (02) 233 1416

Computer People Pty Ltd have offices all over Australia and these are listed below. Computer People Pty Limited is the 'flagship' of the Computer Power Group which has offices in Europe, the UK and America. They can send your details to Australia to save on testing, etc. when you arrive, but you will need to meet with them before they can place you in work.

Sydney	Adelaide	(08) 8232 6455
Level 27	Brisbane	(07) 3368 3840
133 Castlereagh Street	Canberra	(06) 283 6777
Sydney NSW 2000	Darwin	(08) 8981 1614
Australia	Melbourne	(03) 9510 6222
Tel: (02) 261 4900	Perth	(09) 481 0488
Fax: (02) 261 4456		

JKM Consulting place many travellers in positions. They prefer to receive your CV before you arrive and ask that you include your arrival date. JKM Consulting currently has around 400 contractors working in the Sydney region.

JKM Consulting
Level 17, 44 Market Street
Sydney NSW 2000
Tel: (02) 262 1000
Fax: (02) 299 8819

Morgan & Banks Limited is happy to receive CVs before you arrive.

Sydney office	Adelaide	(08) 8212 2677
Level 11, Grosvenor Place	Brisbane	(07) 3221 7433
225 George Street	Canberra	(06) 257 5999
Sydney NSW 2000	Melbourne	(03) 9623 6666
Tel: (02) 256 0333	Perth	(09) 221 2255
Fax: (02) 251 3975		

Morgan & Banks' London office could send your details over for you:

London office
Morgan & Banks Place
Brettenham House
Lancaster Place
London WC2E 7EN
Tel: (0171) 240 1040

Customer sourcing

You can work and earn while you travel on an Aussie Safari. The scheme is called **Programme 2000**.

It's a great opportunity to see the country and meet the people while living with young Australians and other travellers.

Transport, accommodation, food and travel costs are paid for and you also receive a weekly guarantee plus the opportunity to earn good bonuses.

Training is free. You can work for as long as you like but you should be available for at least six to eight weeks.

Independent people can join teams travelling Australia introducing their company to locals and you won't have to sell anything yourself. The teams work the big cities as well as country towns.

Full details and interviews can be arranged in Sydney or Brisbane.

Sydney office
Suite 3, Level 13,
109 Pitt Street
Sydney NSW 2000
Tel: (02) 233 8766

Brisbane office
6th floor,
40 Queen Street
Brisbane QLD 4002
Tel: (07) 3221 6522

Deck hand/cook

It is possible to obtain work on a fishing vessel as a deck hand or cook. This type of work is mostly on prawn trawlers out of Cairns and Townsville in Far North Queensland, Karumba on the Gulf of Carpentaria, Broome in WA and Darwin in the NT.

Most captains prefer to take on an experienced deck hand who will be able to haul nets, sort (grade) and pack prawns (watch out for the spines) and unload the catch. Some knowledge of shipboard safety and first aid is also helpful.

Captains do take on inexperienced travellers but you must commit to the whole season and be prepared for hard work. Unfortunately many travellers go out on the boats thinking that it is a cruise in the sun. It's not.

Most deckhands are paid on a share fisherman basis and not as an employee. You sign a partnership giving you a share in the proceeds of the catch, which technically means you need to fork out money if a loss is made. I have been reassured that this doesn't really happen, but even so, many travellers are opting to be paid a wage instead. Check with the captain what this will be.

You can also take work as a cook on one of the trawlers. You will be responsible for buying supplies and cooking the meals, mostly breakfast and dinner with a light lunch for the crew. Cooks might also be required to help sort the prawns.

There have been stories that females are only taken on board the boats as a recreational activity. Girls should make it very clear that they will not accept this as there is nowhere to go once you're out there, and you will be sharing the sleeping quarters down below. Two female friends could go together, probably working for the one wage.

You should commit yourself for the length of time the boat is at sea or for the season. If you are susceptible to sea sickness this work might not be for you because once you've left port, there's no turning back. The length of time spent out at sea varies from a few weeks to months.

Take one set of wet weather gear, a hat, a beanie if it's cold, suntan lotion and your sea legs.

To find such work you can look in the local papers, go to the pubs where the fisherman drink, go to the docks and ask the captains or leave messages on the noticeboards at the wharves.

In **Townsville**, there are two places to look for work on a prawn trawler. You will need transport to get to them.

Fisherman's Wharf at the end of Seventh Avenue in South Townsville has a noticeboard where you can leave your details.

At the Port Authority at the end of Seventh Avenue (there is another Seventh Avenue a couple of streets along), is a noticeboard where you can leave your details. It does say 'No Entry' to the Port Authority but the board is inside the area at the front of the building.

In **Cairns**, work is seasonal from March to November. Enquire at the Pig Pens, end of Tingarra Street—they're called the Pig Pens because the boats are nosed in like pigs.

Some of the work is also advertised in Saturday's *Cairns Post*.

Karumba is a remote place in the Gulf of Carpentaria. There are two seasons, April 1 to mid-June, and August 1 to December 1. Once you're out to sea, you don't come in during these times.

A company which can arrange for you to work on trawlers out of Karumba is:

Raptis and Son
PO Box 54
Morningside QLD 4170
Fax: (03) 3399 1960

In **Darwin**, the prawn season usually runs from April to May. The time spent at sea varies.

Barra boats also leave from Darwin seven months of the year; most captains make three trips out during this time. You'll find yourself working weird hours, as it depends on when the fish are biting—usually it's at night.

You can find the boats in Darwin moored at a place called **Duck Pond**, at the Francis Bay Drive Marina.

Raptis and Son, details above, also take on crews for their boats leaving from Darwin.

Fishing boats leave from many of the harbours around the country. Check out the local industries of various towns.

Diving instructors

One of the things on the backpacker's agenda while travelling Australia is learning to dive, usually on the Great Barrier Reef. These people need fully qualified diving instructors to teach them.

Qualifications recognised are PADI, SSI, NASDS, NAUI, BASC and AUSI. If you don't have one of these qualifications you may need to do a conversion course.

Positions as diving instructors can be found in many coastal areas of Australia. Travellers often learn to dive in Sydney before heading up the east coast to dive places like the Yongala Wreck off the coast of Townsville or the Cod Hole off the coast of Cairns, or the World Heritage-listed Lord Howe Island. Popular places for travellers to learn to dive include Jervis Bay (on the south coast of NSW), Byron Bay, the Whitsundays, Townsville and Cairns.

To find work, pick up some diving brochures and approach dive companies direct, or look in the yellow pages. You might contact:

Mike Ball Dive Expeditions
252–256 Walker Street
Townsville QLD 4810
Tel: (077) 72 3022
Fax: (077) 21 2152

Pro Dive International
34/330 Wattle Street
Ultimo NSW 2007
Tel: (02) 281 6166
Fax: (02) 281 0660

Farm/station work—jillaroo/jackaroo

Those wishing to experience real outback life might want to try working on a farm or station as a jillaroo, jackaroo, tractor driver, governess or cook.

Many of these outback stations are in Queensland, the Northern Territory and the Kimberley region of Western Australia where a farm size of a million acres is not uncommon. These stations always have other staff, usually young, and often you'll find places have their own helicopters and planes, so they may be remote but not necessarily lonely.

Work in the northern states is mostly available from March to October as during the hot, wet summer months of November to March the stations only maintain a skeleton staff.

Duties will depend on the position you fill and also on what kind of farm/station it is. Stations usually run cattle, and pastoral companies farm wheat and sheep. Experience isn't always necessary but it is useful.

A cook will obviously be cooking, usually breakfast and dinner. If the staff are working on the other side of the farm you might need to prepare lunch for them to take along. Meals are mostly hearty, consisting of meat, meat and more meat, roasts, stews and more meat. A driver's licence is also handy for collecting your food supplies.

Jackaroos and jillaroos will be doing whatever needs doing on the farm, like rounding up stock, either on horseback for cattle or by motorbike for sheep, feeding the stock, drenching stock, mending fences, harvesting crops, etc.

Tractor drivers will be preparing and harvesting crops.

Work is usually a full day of about 12 hours and the mornings start early, with the workers rising at around 5 or 6 am. During the busy times you could find yourself working seven days a week.

Food and accommodation are provided and are usually very basic, either in staff quarters or possibly your own room in the main house. Your salary will be around A$250–A$300 per week after tax. Most backpackers are able to save quite a bit while working on farms/stations, as there is nowhere to go and nothing to spend your money on unless you go into town to kick up your heels.

The clothes you should take include old jeans, long sleeved shirts so as not to get your arms burnt, a wide-brimmed hat or baseball cap, leather gloves which keep hands warm but also have grip, gumboots for the wet weather or Blundstone boots, which are a very sturdy brand of boot, though some workers do wear training shoes. Don't forget your water bottle.

Positions are often found through remote CES offices. Try Alice Springs, Darwin or Mt Isa. Look in newspapers like *The Land* and

Queensland Country Life, and the local papers. These jobs are sometimes advertised on hostel noticeboards, or you could try the following agencies:

Outback Staff & Busy Bodies fill positions mainly on the outback stations of Queensland, the Northern Territory, and the Kimberley area of Western Australia. CVs are accepted before you arrive. They will do a telephone interview before/when you arrive in Australia, and the consultants do like a contact number and a reference if possible.

It is helpful to have done cooking, housekeeping, gardening, or child care work previously. There is also work for experienced horse riders as well as tractor and farm equipment operators.

Outback Staff & Busy Bodies
PO Box 8042
Allenstown QLD 4700
Tel: (079) 27 4300 (Rockhampton)
Fax: (079) 22 6923

PGA Personnel recruits people for rural employment, roadhouses, bars, hotel staff, etc. for Western Australia and the Northern Territory.
PGA Personnel
3/277 Great Eastern Highway
Belmont WA 6104
Tel: (09) 479 4544
Fax: (09) 277 7311

Rural Enterprises supplies the rural sectors of Western Australia and the Northern Territory with competent agricultural staff.

There is quite a lot of work for experienced tractor drivers of harvesters, combines, etc.

The busiest times in Western Australia are during seeding time in April/May/June, and during harvest time from mid-October to Christmas, but this does depend on the rains.

CVs will be accepted before you arrive.
Rural Enterprises
326 Hay Street
Perth WA 6000
Tel: (09) 325 8411
Fax: (09) 221 4558

Those who would like to work on a farm or station can join the **Visitoz Scheme**. This training programme invites students and backpackers to gain a taste of outback farm or station life as a working jackaroo or jillaroo.

The scheme is run by Dan and Joanna Burnet on their working 510 hectare cattle property, Springbrook Host Farm, which is about 280 km north west of Brisbane—a bus from Brisbane passes the gate five times a week in each direction and will stop on request.

Training at Springbrook, or one of the associate farms, over the four days covers tractor operation, ag-bike and horse riding, cattle handling and useful skills such as fencing and scrub clearing. Once you have completed the course the Burnets will offer you a choice of the suitable jobs available. You will need to pay your own travel expenses to get to your first job, but they are often refunded by the employer when you arrive.

You will need a sunhat, boots, alarm clock, penknife and suntan lotion, so include the purchase of these items in your budget as they are cheaper if you obtain them in rural Australia. Passport-size photos for your student ID card are also necessary.

In Australia contact:
Dan and Joanna Burnet
Springbrook,
via Goomeri 4601 QLD
Tel/Fax: (071) 686 106

To arrange a position with the scheme in the UK before you leave for Australia, contact:
William Taunton-Burnet
21 Harleyford Road
London SE11 5AX
Tel: (0171) 735 2559
Fax: (0171) 820 8686
Mobile: 0385 288 779

There is a non-refundable application fee of £10 and once you are accepted the placement fee of £340 is payable. This covers five days of tuition as well as being met at Brisbane airport on arrival, assistance with the completion of the necessary paperwork (bank account, tax file number, Medicare card, etc.) and a chance to get over jet lag in reasonable surroundings with a saltwater swimming pool to cool off in.

Hospitality

Hospitality is a growing industry in Australia and it covers a whole gamut of positions in places ranging from cafes to five star hotels/resorts.

The variety of employment available includes kitchen hands, canteen staff, housekeepers, waiters/waitresses, bar staff, reception staff, qualified chefs and valets.

Experience is required at most establishments, though sometimes you can be taken on if you have the correct personality.

It is advised that you bring your own work clothes and tools if you're hoping to gain a position in the hospitality industry, but you can buy uniforms and utensils from suppliers in Australia.

Waiters/waitresses will need full black and whites and the waiter's friend, a bottle opener.

Chefs should bring their uniform and their knives.

Work can be found in the major cities, in popular holiday areas such as the Gold Coast and on island resorts, in ski resorts and resorts in the outback. You can find work by knocking on doors, contacting the human resources departments of major hotels, casinos, etc. looking in the papers or contacting one of the agencies below.

The Allseasons Hospitality Recruitment places those with experience and/or qualifications in hospitality positions in Sydney, and is affiliated with agencies in Victoria and Queensland. Contact them at:

The Allseasons Hospitality Recruitment
330 Wattle Street
Ultimo NSW 2007
Tel: (02) 212 5466
Fax: (02) 212 6946

Bensons Hospitality & Training

Sydney	**Cairns:** (070) 412 233
52 Phillip Street	**Melbourne:** (03) 9348 9277
Sydney NSW 2000	
Tel: (02) 247 7888	

Black and White Brigade
This agency places those with experience and/or qualifications in hospitality positions in Sydney, Brisbane and Melbourne.

Sydney office	**Brisbane office**
6a Gray Street	5/433 Ipswich Road
Bondi Junction NSW 2022	Annerley QLD 4103
Tel: (02) 369 4044	Tel: (07) 3848 3437
Fax: (02) 369 1270	Fax: (07) 3848 6086

Melbourne office
Ground office 3
620 St Kilda Road
Melbourne VIC 3004
Tel: (03) 9525 0599
Fax: (03) 9525 0611

On the Gold Coast try:

Power Personnel has been established on the Gold Coast for 25 years and gives the personal approach to hospitality positions. Good for a chat.

Power Personnel
Level 5, 38 Cavill Avenue
Surfers Paradise QLD 4217
Tel: (07) 5527 5800
Fax: (07) 5592 4230

In Cairns (Queensland) try:

VIP Hospitality Services
Level 1, 129 Abbott Street
Cairns QLD 4870
Tel: (070) 317 881
Fax: (070) 316 719

Also see the section under 'Resort Work'.

Journalism and photography

Many magazines and newspapers rely on freelance contributions to fill their pages. Travel editors in particular are always looking for well-written articles accompanied by photographs. If you've read these pages and think you could write something too, then you most probably can, because you don't necessarily need to be a qualified journalist or photographer to supply articles or photos.

If you've been on a trip and wish to pass on your experience or tips, there are magazines and newspapers out there that would be interested. The backpacker ones especially like to print helpful hints for travellers. Those glossy magazines and newspapers on the news stands also rely on freelance contributions to enhance their travel pages.

It is necessary to supply typed text, which is hard to do on the road—I know—maybe you could use a computer at your workplace in your lunch hour.

If you are serious about supplying articles, research your market by obtaining copies of relevant newspapers and magazines and examine the style they use. Then get writing!

There are several books which list the various markets and how to get started. These can be found in or near the reference section of most bookshops.

There are also agencies which will handle your articles and distribute them for you. They are often mentioned in the market guides referred to above, but I do believe they take a 50% cut from any article sold.

Stock agencies will sell your photographs for you. You may find your shots in travel brochures, on postcards, on calendars or in magazines. Popular shots include photos of couples and families enjoying themselves on beaches.

I don't know if you'll get rich from supplying freelance articles and photographs but it is a buzz to see your name in print. You never know, you might end up with memoirs, a coffee-table picture book or a travel guide!

Legal

The work available in the legal field will be mainly as office support or as a paralegal. Overseas solicitors need to sit exams to obtain their practicing certificate in Australia and due to the time involved they usually find work as paralegals instead.

Legal secretaries and WP operators should have at least two years' experience and knowledge of a Windows package, particularly Microsoft Word, Word Perfect or Word Perfect 5.1. Most of the positions are for regular business hours, though there are some large legal firms with 24-hour typing pools where you may obtain morning or afternoon work. The rate of pay for legal secretaries and WP operators is around A$18 per hour.

Paralegals can do a variety of work from filing, chronological document sorting or document discovery to research and document management. The rate for paralegals is around A$14 per hour.

The length of your employment in the legal field can vary from a day to several weeks or months.

The courts close for a two-month break in January and February but I have been advised that work is still available during this time.

The agencies to contact for legal work include:

ADIA Centacom Law Appointments will accept letters from overseas but will need to meet with you before they can place you in a position.
> **Sydney**
> Level 2, 280 George Street
> Sydney NSW 2000
> Tel: (02) 231 6622
> Fax: (02) 223 4626

Law Staff (NSW) Pty Ltd place travellers in legal positions and will accept your details from overseas, but they will expect to meet you on your arrival in Australia before placing you in a position. You can find them at:
> **Law Staff (NSW) Pty Ltd**
> Level 14, 115 Pitt Street (near Wynyard station)
> Sydney NSW 2000
> Tel: (02) 235 3399
> Fax: (02) 235 3070

Learned Friends have been operating for 11 years and will accept your CV before you arrive, but you will need to meet them before they can place you in a position. Look out for the London office of Learned Friends opening in March 1996. The staff there will be able to advise you about working through their Sydney office.
> **Learned Friends**
> Level 5, 191 Clarence Street
> Sydney NSW 2000
> Tel: (02) 262 5858
> Fax: (02) 262 5875

Nursing

There are various levels at which you can nurse in Australia. At the top end of the scale you have RNs (Registered Nurses) who are fully qualified nurses working in various areas of the hospitals and who can administer drugs. Then you have ENs (Enrolled Nurses) who work in extended care facilities and cannot administer drugs. Next are the AINs (Assistants In Nursing) or PCs (Personal Carers) who work under supervision in nursing homes.

To work as an RN in Australia you need to be registered in the state where you wish to work. Agencies have advised me that the easiest and cheapest way to obtain registration is to contact one of the registration boards below and find out their exact requirements, then on your arrival obtain your registration.

Once you are registered to nurse in one state you can roll it over to any other state, except for Western Australia. Check the various requirements from the different registration boards.

New South Wales
Nurses Registration Board
PO Box K599
Haymarket NSW 2000
Tel: (02) 281 4300

Victoria
Chief Executive Officer
Nurses Board of Victoria
GPO Box 4932
Melbourne VIC 3001
Tel: (03) 9613 0333

South Australia
Chief Executive Officer
Nurses Board of SA
PO Box 7176
Hutt Street
Adelaide SA 5000
Tel: (08) 8223 2630

Queensland
Executive Officer
Qld. Nurses Registration Board
GPO Box 2928
Brisbane QLD 4001
Tel: (07) 3234 1402

Western Australia
Chief Executive Officer
Nurses Board of WA
PO Box 336
Nedlands WA 6009
Tel: (09) 386 8656

Northern Territory
Registrar
Nurses Board of the NT
GPO Box 4221
Darwin NT 0801
Tel: (089) 99 2948

Once registration is obtained you can either register with an agency or approach local hospitals directly to be listed on their casual pools. Bring a CV detailing your training and experience, plus original and back-up copies of your certificates and registration with you.

Agencies mostly supply staff to hospitals in specific areas. You might consider registering with an agency in your area first, because without your own transport, getting to work might prove to be a problem. Postings are usually found in the major cities, though work can be offered in the country areas. Those nurses with specialised skills, ICU, A&E and CCU, are in demand. The length of time you are employed at each position may vary from a day to a few months.

Registered nurses can expect to receive around A$15 per hour plus penalty rates and a shift allowance; you should be paid weekly or fortnightly.

In the southern states the busy months are from June to September. Many nurses go on holidays during this time, and it is also the winter season with more people getting sick. Work slackens off a little around December/January as the surgeons often take time off during this period.

Uniforms vary from hospital to hospital and from one state to another, but a plain white uniform should stand you in good stead. In Victoria though, the norm is a pair of blue pants or a skirt with a white shirt. Your agency or hospital will be able to advise you on this.

To find work, look in the phone book for hospitals and employment agencies. Agencies also advertise in the papers and backpacker magazines, or you could try one of the following, just a sample of the many agencies available.

In New South Wales (Sydney) try:

ADIA Centacom Health Staff
83 Mount Street
North Sydney NSW 2060
Tel: (02) 9956 8877

Centennial Nurses supply nurses to hospitals in Sydney's Eastern Suburbs. They also have an office in Melbourne.
Sydney
34 Queen's Park Road
Bondi Junction NSW 2022
Tel: (02) 369 4325

Drake Medox
Sydney   **Melbourne** (03) 9245 0210
Level 12, 60 Margaret Street
Sydney NSW 2000
Tel: (02) 241 4488
Fax: (02) 247 5993

Eastern Suburbs Nursing Service supplies nurses to hospitals in the metropolitan area and also to private patients at homes/hospitals. You will be able to contact them at:
Eastern Suburbs Nursing Service
35 Wentworth Street
Randwick NSW 2031
Tel: (02) 314 6365
Fax: (02) 398 7401

Gordon Nurses supplies nurses to hospitals on Sydney's North Shore.
214 Military Road
Neutral Bay NSW 2089
Tel: (02) 9953 9388
Fax: (02) 9953 3824

Medistaff supply nurses to hospitals throughout the city and to some country areas as well.
   Sydney
   1st Floor, 349 Pacific Highway
   North Sydney NSW 2060
   Tel: (02) 9957 5666   Toll-free number within Australia:
   Fax: (07) 9957 5900   1800 676 856

In Queensland (Brisbane) try:

Finns Nursing Agency is run by an Irish couple and therefore places many Irish travellers in nursing positions throughout Brisbane's hospitals, and can find postings for nurses of other nationalities as well. The agency also supplies nurses to tourist resorts and the Queensland outback. They can help you find accommodation and will accept mail addressed to you there and forward it on to you if you go off travelling. They can be contacted at:
   Finns Nursing Agency
   4th Floor, 139 Leichhardt Street
   Spring Hill QLD 4004
   Tel: (07) 3832 0170
   Fax: (07) 3832 4590

Queensland Nursing is a long-established agency in Queensland. It pays weekly wages and supplies nurses (RNs, ENs and AINs) to hospitals and nursing homes throughout the Brisbane area and occasionally to country hospitals too. Jennie Cross, Director of the agency, is always happy to assist nurses from overseas who are seeking work in or around Brisbane. The agency can be reached at:
   Queensland Nursing
   9 Shadowood Street
   Kenmore Hills QLD 4069
   Tel: (07) 3374 2097
   Fax: (07) 3374 2410

In Queensland (Cairns) try:

Cairns Nursing Agency supplies Cairns' hospitals and nursing homes, and staffs hospitals in Queensland country regions and those located in remote areas.
   Cairns Nursing Agency
   PO Box 2137
   Cairns QLD 4870
   Tel: (070) 54 2739   Fax: (070) 33 1255

In Victoria (Melbourne) try:

ADIA Centacom Health Staff
Melbourne (03) 9699 5055

Centennial Nurses
Unit 7, 150 Beach Road
Sandringham VIC 3191
Tel: (03) 9598 1554

Medistaff supply nurses to Melbourne's hospitals.
1st Floor, 608 St. Kilda Road
Melbourne VIC 3004
Tel: (03) 9510 1444
Fax: (03) 9510 2155

In Western Australia (Perth) try:

Meditemp supplies nurses to hospitals in Perth, most country hospitals, remote communities and mine sites.
Perth
26 Charles Street
South Perth WA 6151
Tel: (09) 474 3043
Fax: (09) 367 7690

In South Australia (Adelaide) try:

ADIA Centacom Health Staff
Adelaide (08) 8271 1488

Medstaff
32 Grenfell Street
Adelaide SA 5000
Tel: (08) 8212 4755
Fax: (08) 8231 9228

Office support

Office support encompasses filing, clerical work, data entry, word processing and typing, as well as the work done by a telephonist, receptionist, secretary and personal assistant.

Skills required include audio, shorthand, a typing speed of at least

50–60 words per minute and the ability to use a number of packages, keystrokes of 10,000–12,000 per hour and experience on a switchboard. The more versatile your skills, the more positions you could be offered and the rate you receive should be higher as well.

If you don't have the skills listed above don't be put off registering with agencies; a fashion buyer friend of mine with a slow typing speed was offered work doing data entry and filing. Agencies do like you to have as many skills as possible as it makes you more marketable, but positions at a variety of levels do become available, and my friend is living proof. Staff who are able to operate Windows packages are in real demand, particularly those with experience on Word for Windows and Word Perfect for Windows. An increasing number of secretarial positions require you to have a basic knowledge of spreadsheet programs, so knowledge of Lotus 123, Excel or Powerpoint is a real bonus and will aid your marketability. If you don't have any experience with these packages but you have used others, agencies will often provide cross training programs.

The length of time you are employed for at each position can vary. It is essential to stay near a phone so you can take work as soon as it is offered, or else ring your agency regularly.

You can expect to receive around A$12/13 an hour for data entry and around A$14/15 an hour for secretarial work. Legal and medical secretaries are often required and with a couple of years' experience under your belt you can expect to receive a few dollars more per hour.

Corporate dress is required for most office work, though as I have mentioned before dress up the first day, see what everyone else is wearing, and if the office has a more relaxed dress code then you can fit yourself out accordingly. As long as you are neat and tidy (that means ironed clothes), you should be okay.

To find office-based work, look in the Saturday papers or contact one of the agencies listed below. They place travellers in positions and have offices all over the country.

You might like to obtain a free postcode book from the Post Office, as one thing many secretaries have trouble with is the spelling of the place names in addresses—visitors' interpretations of Australian place names can cause great amusement.

Alectus Personnel Pty Ltd
Sydney
Level 10, 280 George Street
Sydney NSW 2000
Tel: (02) 223 2155
Fax: (02) 223 0082

Adelaide (08) 8212 2944
Brisbane (07) 3236 2244
Canberra (06) 257 8111
Melbourne (03) 9654 1777

Work opportunities

Bligh Appointments was first established in London in 1974 and employs many working holidaymakers commuting between Sydney and London. See the 'Accounting' section for their contact details.

Centacom has a large employment network servicing the major capital cities and many suburban areas.

Sydney	**Adelaide**	(08)	8271 1422
Level 9, 275 George Street	**Brisbane**	(07)	3221 31855
Sydney NSW 2000	**Canberra**	(06)	247 8622
Tel: (02) 231 5555	**Darwin**	(089)	41 09 14
Fax: (02) 299 2063	**Melbourne**	(03)	9654 6154
	Perth	(09)	221 4642
	Hobart	(002)	34 8999

Drake Personnel has offices in 11 countries around the world including France, Canada, the UK (20 branches) and New Zealand.

They also have a Drake International Passport which can help simplify the registration process.

Sydney	**Adelaide**	(08)	8212 4141
Level 12, 60 Margaret Street	**Brisbane**	(07)	3221 6099
Sydney NSW 2000	**Canberra**	(06)	281 1022
Tel: (02) 241 4488	**Darwin**	(089)	810 020
Fax: (02) 247 5993	**Melbourne**	(03)	9245 0245
	Perth	(09)	321 9911
	Hobart	(002)	243 399

Ecco Personnel has offices throughout the country which place working holidaymakers in office-based positions.

Sydney	**Adelaide**	(08)	8231 4747
Level 6, 109 Pitt Street	**Brisbane**	(07)	3229 4222
Sydney NSW 2000	**Canberra**	(06)	286 2177
Tel: (02) 221 5955	**Melbourne**	(03)	670 0800
Fax: (02) 221 5164	**Perth**	(09)	472 1755

Julia Ross Personnel has five branches in Australia specialising in appointments for temporary and permanent staff. Feel free to forward your resume prior to reaching Australia. Your details will then be kept on file pending your arrival at their offices, although they do recommend that you keep your CV with you until you register with them in Australia.

Sydney	**Brisbane**	(07)	3236 2233
Level 12, 115 Pitt Street	**Melbourne**	(03)	9650 4433
Sydney NSW 2000			
Tel: (02) 232 1911			
Fax: (02) 232 1748			

Key People and **Commercial Computer Centre** are data entry specialists. They require their staff to have had at least two years' experience in the workforce and a typing speed of at least 12,000 keystrokes per hour on both alpha and numeric systems, and be at least 95% accurate. They have both short-term and long-term temporary positions available.

Sydney	**Adelaide** (08)	8332 5322
Level 3, 418A Elizabeth Street	**Brisbane** (07)	3391 4588
Surry Hills NSW 2010	**Canberra** (06)	251 5133
Tel: (02) 212 7458	**Melbourne** (03)	9615 8888
Fax: (02) 211 0115	**Perth** (09)	324 1275

Manpower require skilled office staff, word processor operators, data entry clerks and secretaries to fill their temporary jobs.

Sydney
Level 9, 34 Hunter Street
Sydney NSW 2000
Tel: (02) 231 4844
Fax: (02) 235 0097

Brisbane (07) 3221 0766

Metier Personnel is a specialist consultancy agency providing travellers with work in office support positions. There are branches all over Australia.

Sydney	**Adelaide** (08)	8231 0820
Level 11, Chifley Tower	**Brisbane** (07)	3839 5011
2 Chifley Square	**Canberra** (06)	257 6344
Sydney NSW 2000	**Melbourne** (03)	9614 2443
Tel: (02) 233 7188	**Perth** (09)	322 5198
Fax: (02) 221 4347		

Select Appointments

Sydney	**Brisbane** (07)	3221 1500
109 Pitt Street	**Melbourne** (03)	9629 2399
Sydney NSW 2000	**Perth** (09)	321 3133
Tel: (02) 206 2200		
Fax: (02) 206 2214		

Temporary Solutions places many travellers in office support and accounting positions. See the section headed 'Accounting' for their details.

Western Staff Services have 400 offices worldwide and are happy to place travellers in office support positions. See the 'Accounting' section for contact details.

Resort work

There are many resorts throughout Australia and all of them require staff to keep them running smoothly. Much of the work is hospitality-related. The most popular areas with travellers are Queensland's island resorts, the outback areas of Kakadu and Ayers Rock/Uluru and at the ski resorts in the south-east.

Queensland island resorts

There are many islands along the Queensland coast, most of them un-inhabited. Those which have been developed as resorts offer work to the traveller.

Most resorts prefer experienced people, though inexperienced people can be taken on as there is often a high turnover of staff. Personality is vital in obtaining this work, as you will be dealing with people.

High season for resort work is during the winter months when the Aussies living in the south head northwards for the warmer weather. School holidays are also busy times, especially over the 6-week break in the summer.

Work can be found as housemaids, waiting staff for food and beverages, silver service, wine service, breakfast service, room attendants, kitchen hands, chefs-commis, demis and chef-de-parties, breakfast chefs, sous chefs, pastry chefs, a-la-carte, porters, etc.

Most of the work is shift work and you will be required to stay on the island until your day off. Accommodation is provided on the island but you are usually charged a rental fee of about A$80. Meals are included, but you should check if this applies to all your meals or only those you eat while you're on duty. If it's the latter, you will have to buy some of your own meals. Having your own work clothes is handy, though most resorts have their own uniform.

Staff are usually allowed to use guest facilities like gym equipment, swimming pools, bars, etc. when they are off duty, though some of the islands provide staff facilities.

There are various ways to find work on island resorts. Look in the local papers, on hostel noticeboards and at CES offices. CES offices to try for work on the resorts include:

Gladstone CES   for work on Heron Island
Mackay CES   for work on Lindeman and Brampton Islands
Bundaberg CES   for work on Lady Elliott Island

You could also try the following:

Australian Resorts is the operator of Great Keppel, Brampton, Dunk,

Bedarra and Lizard Islands.

Professionals with experience are preferred and an Australian national would be given preference over a holidaymaker on a working visa.

Enquire about the availability of work by fax or write, including your CV and references, to:

Recruitment Manager
Australian Resorts
PO Box 1033
Brisbane QLD 4001.
Fax: (07) 3360 2437

Whitsunday Personnel: There are over 70 islands in the Whitsunday group. Six of these have resorts on them. They are: Hayman, Hamilton, Long, South Molle, Daydream and Lindeman Islands. The resorts vary in the degrees of luxury they offer, and also in the types of positions they require to be filled.

Work can be found at the resorts through **Cannonvale CES** or try:
Whitsunday Personnel
1st Floor, Beach Plaza
Airlie Beach QLD 4802
Tel: (079) 465 539

For work in resorts off Townsville and Cairns try the CES, **Black and White Brigade** and **VIP Hospitality**. You'll find their contact details listed in the 'Hospitality' section.

Outback resorts

The two areas with outback resorts are Ayers Rock/Uluru and Kakadu. There is a high turnover of staff and travellers are often taken on as there is no local population to draw on for employment. A 'remote' allowance is usually offered to entice staff to stay.

High season is during the school holidays and also the winter months, when it is the best time to visit the outback.

Housemaids, waiters and chefs are often required.

The use of the resort facilities is usually allowed. Staff have to make their own entertainment, because Ayers Rock/Uluru and Kakadu are remote areas. After you've seen the main sights, what else is there to do?

I recommend that you organise your work before you arrive in the area, otherwise you will have to find your own accommodation until a position arises. Accommodation is provided once you have a position.

To find work at the resorts, try the CES offices in **Alice Springs** and **Darwin**. You can also try the employment agencies found in the Yellow Pages. Pick up travel brochures and contact recruitment officers directly.

Ski resorts

There are some great skiing areas in Australia and during the ski season, which officially begins with the long weekend in June and ends on the long weekend in October, people are required to work in the resorts and shops.

The skiing region is located on the slopes of the Snowy Mountains in NSW and Victoria.

In NSW the skiing areas are: Thredbo, Perisher-Smiggins, Mt. Selwyn, Blue Cow-Guthega and Charlotte's Pass.

In Victoria the skiing areas are: Mt Buller, Fall's Creek and Mt Hotham.

The positions available cover a broad range of skills but are mostly in and/or related to the hospitality industry. They include: cooks/chefs, drinks persons, kitchen hands, food and beverage waiters, sales staff in ski hire shops, housemaids, performers, reception staff, etc. Mechanically minded people are required on the slopes to operate lifts, etc.

Calls for workers go out in the major papers in March to attract the itinerant, and notices go out to the CES in April/May. It is preferred that you are available to work for the whole season.

You will need to fill in an application form and send your CV, references and an ID photo, then play a waiting game. All the applications are sorted through and as so many people apply for positions each season, those with experience are snapped up first. If it is an incredibly good season you might pick something up even if you lack the necessary experience.

I have heard that if you miss out on a position, it is a good idea to try again after the second or third week. People often drop out at this time for varying reasons—maybe bits have unexpectedly fallen off because of the cold.

The demand for staff also depends on the white stuff. If bumper snowfalls occur then there will be an increase in staff to cater for the hordes which head for the snow fields.

Accommodation is usually included—it depends on the employer though—plus a wage, as is food and possibly a ski pass too. Yee ha!

To find work on the New South Wales slopes contact **Cooma CES** on (064) 521 788. For work on the Victorian slopes try **Wangaratta CES** on (057) 221 477.

Another way to obtain work is to pick up all the snow brochures from a travel agent and contact personnel managers at individual chalets/resorts and restaurants. Also look in the local papers.

Roadhouses

Roadhouses are basically places to fill up the old petrol tank and have something to eat. They are found all over Australia and are situated as you approach town or as you leave town and—sometimes, they *are* town.

Food on offer ranges from fast food over-the-counter, to meals in sit-down restaurants. Staff are required to cook and serve these meals and sometimes someone is required to fill the petrol tanks.

Most backpackers who find work in a roadhouse have lobbed into town, decided they liked the place and wanted to stay. Due to the remoteness of some of the roadhouses, they are a good place to save that pay packet for future travels.

Securing work is usually a matter of asking over the counter if help is required. Sometimes jobs are advertised in the CES or in the local paper but the best way is to enquire within.

In Western Australia you might contact **PGA** (see the section under 'Farm/station work' for their details), as they sometimes place people in roadhouse positions.

Scientific/lab staff

Bench work is available for lab technicians, analysts and chemists in the mining, chemical, biochemical, biotechnology, environmental, pharmaceutical, food and beverage industries.

Having a degree isn't always the basis on which you will be placed, as industry-specific experience followed by instrument skills are the most valued qualifications in the industry. HPLC skills are highly regarded; people with these skills are in great demand. Computer literacy is also helpful. Flexibility is the key to finding work as specialised skills in one area will see you in good stead in another area.

The time length of the available positions can vary, but the longer you can commit yourself the better. You may find you're only required for a day or two, or you might be needed to see a project to its completion.

Rates of pay can range from $10–20 per hour and depend on the skills required of you.

Labstaff Pty Ltd is Australia's largest scientific agency and places many travellers in temporary positions all over the country.

Sydney office	**Adelaide** (08)	8361 2366
Suite 402, 77 Berry Street	**Melbourne** (03)	9820 9011

North Sydney NSW 2060
Tel: (02) 9957 3544
Fax: (02) 9957 6282

Perth (09) 322 7688
Brisbane (07) 3870 9977

Teaching

Finding casual teaching work in Australia isn't an easy process when you are foreign-trained. Firstly you need to have your qualifications recognised, and secondly, you need to register in the state where you want to work. Each state has different requirements.

If you want to find out about having your qualifications recognised and becoming registered in a particular state, then contact **NOOSR** (National Office of Overseas Skills Recognition), as they produce a brochure to advise people about the process. Australian Consulates/High Commissions may also carry this brochure.

NOOSR
GPO Box 1407
Canberra ACT 2601

Unfortunately there are no agencies which can place you in temporary teaching positions. The way to find work is by directly contacting those schools which have casual teaching pools. If you have no transport you will need to contact schools close to where you are living.

Australia is a popular place for people to come and learn English. For those who have the RSA/Cambridge Certificate in TEFL (Teaching English as a Foreign Language), you could get into this lucrative market and teach individuals on a one-to-one basis, or work through one of the private language schools.

All teaching schools have to be accredited and most of them belong to ELICOS (English Language Intensive Courses to Overseas Students). If you contact them they can supply you with a list of their members. You could then contact the school where you'd like to work.

ELICOS
PO Box 30
Pyrmont NSW 2009
Tel: +61 2 660 6455
Fax: +61 2 566 2230

Technical, industrial, trades and unskilled work

Technical, industrial, trades and unskilled work covers many professions in a variety of industries.

Technical positions include: engineers, draughtsmen, architects, computer people, inspectors, tracers, etc.

Industrial positions include: store people, forklift operators, drivers, stocktakers, carpenters, fitters, riggers, etc.

Trade positions include: electricians, boilermakers, painters, riggers, plumbers, toolmakers, carpenters, welders, etc.

Unskilled positions include: labourers, process workers, store people, dock hands, etc.

Work can be found in a range of industries including manufacturing, mining, building and construction, transportation, warehousing, etc.

When you're looking for work make sure you bring all your trade certificates, etc. and possibly some tools, though most agencies can lend you tools. You will need steel-capped boots (if that is what's appropriate to your profession) and work clothes.

Australia doesn't recognise overseas qualifications in some professions, such as electrical qualifications, but don't worry, you can still find work as an assistant in your field. The length of time you're required at each job can vary, and it depends on how long it takes to get the job done.

Unskilled work is often found by word of mouth or by turning up at building sites. Look in the papers as well or contact one of the following agencies which often place travellers in positions at varying levels:

ADIA Centacom Industrial
  Parramatta
  Level 7, 80 George Street
  Parramatta NSW 2150
  Tel: (02) 689 3055
  Fax: (02) 635 9020

  Adelaide (08) 8271 1499
  Brisbane (07) 3347 3877
  Melbourne (03) 9699 1011
  Perth (09) 322 3112

ADIA Value Engineering
  Sydney
  280 George Street
  Sydney NSW 2000
  Tel: (02) 231 6311
  Fax: (02) 231 3531

  Adelaide (08) 8271 1411
  Brisbane (07) 3229 8488
  Melbourne (03) 9822 8666
  Perth (09) 322 2211

Bligh Appointments is an Australian owned company which employs many working holidaymakers commuting between Sydney and London. See the 'Accounting' section for their contact details.

Drake Industrial
Sydney
Level 3, 191 Clarence Street
Sydney NSW 2000
Tel: (02) 262 1755
Fax: (02) 299 1238

Adelaide	(08)	8231 7233
Brisbane	(07)	3379 3411
Gold Coast	(07)	5591 2004
Melbourne	(03)	3696 6044
Perth	(09)	322 4022

Ecco Personnel Industrial
Parramatta
Level 3, 239 Church Street
Parramatta NSW 2150
Tel: (02) 891 3294
Fax: (02) 891 1485

Adelaide	(08)	8231 4747
Brisbane	(07)	3229 4222
Canberra	(06)	286 2177
Melbourne	(03)	9670 0800
Perth	(09)	472 1755

Ecco Personnel Technical
Suite 403, Level 4, 83 Mount Street
North Sydney NSW 2060
Tel: (02) 9929 8522
Fax: (02) 9954 4391

Forstaff
Sydney
15 Frank Street
Wetherill Park NSW 2164
Tel: (02) 757 4888
Fax: (02) 757 2520

Adelaide	(08)	8364 2200
Brisbane	(07)	3278 0200
Melbourne	(03)	9568 4011

Skilled Work Force
Sydney
Level 1,
221-229 Sydney Park Road
Alexandria NSW 2015
Tel: (02) 581 8899
Fax: (02) 559 1043

Adelaide	(08)	8340 1288
Brisbane	(07)	3369 7199
Darwin	(089)	84 4067
Hobart	(002)	73 3448
Melbourne	(03)	9699 4199
Perth	(09)	361 7455

Western Staff Services have 400 offices worldwide and are happy to place travellers in light and heavy industrial positions. See the 'Accounting' section for their contact details.

Travel consultants

Travel consultants are always in demand in Australia, especially from mid-January to mid-October. Those of you with knowledge of the universally recognised SABRE and GALILEO won't have a problem finding work.

Length of positions vary between 2–8 weeks on average with the same employer.

Agencies which can help find you work in the travel industry are listed below:

Travel Personnel: This agency has work throughout Sydney. Travellers are also in demand for positions throughout the country as they don't have commitments such as a boy/girl friend or a lease to tie them down and are happy to take off to fill a position, say, in Alice Springs.

Travel Personnel will accept your CV, references and certificates before you arrive. If you come from the UK you could contact their associate office in London, which can forward your details for you.

Sydney office	**Travel Job Shop (London office)**
Level 4, 115 Pitt Street	17 Woodstock Street
Sydney NSW 2000	London W1R 1HE
Tel: (02) 9223 9955	Tel: (0171) 629 1903
Fax: (02) 9223 9338	Fax: (0171) 629 0266

Waiting

Waiting on tables is a universal profession and Australia has many eateries ranging from small cafes to large restaurants.

The easiest way to find work is to walk into an establishment and ask if anything is going. There are also agencies which can place you in waiting positions, mostly for function work or silver service. Refer to the 'Hospitality', 'Roadhouse' and 'Resort Work' sections.

7 Holidaying

Australia is a very large island with vastly varied terrain and weather patterns. It offers you, the working holidaymaker, many opportunities to discover just how diverse it is for yourself.

You will have in mind just what you want to see and do, but Australia is more than the Great Barrier Reef, the Outback and Sydney Harbour. This section is designed to help you decide just what you can see and how to see it.

As many people begin their time in Sydney, this seems like a perfect place to start.

Sightseeing Sydney

Everyone spends time in Sydney where there is plenty to see and do, and extensive transport systems to help you see and do it all.

If you want to hit the tourist trail but don't feel too energetic, then you might like to catch the red **Explorer Bus** which is the hop-on hop-off bus taking in all the sights of the city. There is also the blue **Bondi and Bay Explorer** which takes you to the famous bays and beaches.

Transport around Sydney

Buses, trains and ferries make up the Sydney System which keeps Sydney moving. There is no smoking on the transport system.

The buses

The blue and white buses cover the city and many of the suburbs.

Buses to the north of the city leave from the Wynyard Park terminal in York Street, (outside Wynyard train station). Buses to the south, west and east of the city leave from Circular Quay.

Tickets

Tickets are priced according to the number of zones you will be travelling through. You can only buy single and return tickets from bus drivers, who prefer you to have small change for the fare.

There are various passes available including the **BusTripper** which is an all-day ticket allowing you to hop on and off the blue and white State Transit buses—good for sightseeing! There is also the 7-day **TravelPass** which can be used when you start work. Another ticket is the **TravelTen** which allows ten rides through the sections of your choice. These tickets can be bought from some newsagents on the bus routes, some train stations and at Circular Quay.

To use the magnetic strip tickets you must dip them in the green ticket reader as you enter the bus.

You board the bus through the front door. To get off you press the button, which alerts the driver to stop at the next stop. You alight from the door in the middle. You'll learn!

Nightride Bus Network

Between midnight and 5 am Nightride buses operate. They all leave from Town Hall and you can use your return or weekly ticket on them, or buy a Nightride bus ticket from the driver.

The bus routes and timetables are on the back of the train timetables.

To find out more about the buses visit the information centres in Martin Place—it's at the top end of Martin Place, so if you are near the Cenotaph then you're at the wrong end—and at Circular Quay.

The trains (CityRail)

The trains travel around the city, go out to most suburbs and can take you as far west as the Blue Mountains, up north to the Hunter Valley and down south to Bomaderry. There are eight colour-coded routes. They run from around 5 in the morning until about 12.30 in the evening. If you miss the last train home you can catch the Nightride bus service referred to previously.

Trains travel underground in the city, but elsewhere they are above ground.

Most trains are four to eight carriages long and are either silver double deckers or the new air conditioned Tangaras; both have doors that open automatically. When waiting for a train, stand behind the yellow line. You should also stand clear of the doors to let the exiting passengers alight first before you get on board yourself.

After 8 pm the **Nightsafe** service begins. Inside the yellow line you will notice 'Nightsafe area' written on the platform in blue. This is where the Nightsafe carriages will stop. Even though the train may have many carriages only two will be Nightsafe. They are near the guards' compartment which is recognised by a blue light. Nightsafe trains are for your safety as the number of people riding trains dramatically decreases at night. If you find yourself in trouble there is a help button near the door which links you with the guard or the driver.

So if you're coming home late and find the carriage door won't open and the carriage is in darkness, you'll know why.

Heavy fines are imposed on those who don't buy a ticket. At the time of publication it was A$100. Many inspectors patrol the trains.

Track work is often done on weekends. If a station or an area of track is closed, a bus service is put on instead.

Using the escalators

The underground city train stations have long escalators that take you to the station. When using them, stand to the left, or walk up/down on the right. People get annoyed if you block this passage and you will definitely be showing you are a tourist if you do this.

Tickets

Stations are becoming electronic so at most of them you can buy a ticket with a magnetic strip from a machine. There is usually a ticket window open to purchase a ticket or if you need help.

The machines take coins and some notes (a picture on the front of the machine will show which notes are accepted) and are easy to use once you know how. Follow the message at the top of the machine. First select your destination (these are listed in alphabetical order), then choose what type of ticket you want (single, return, etc.) A message will advise you how much the ticket is. If you decide not to proceed, cancel what you've done, or put your money in and a ticket will be printed for you.

There are various tickets available including the single and return which must be used on the same day and the seven-day **RailPass** (known as a 'weekly'). The cost depends on how many zones you will be travelling through. TravelPasses can also be bought if you will be using a combination of bus, train and ferry travel. Off-peak tickets (bought after 9.00 am weekdays and any time on weekends) are much cheaper than peak travel tickets. A **CityHopper** ticket which allows you to hop on and off the trains in the city can also be purchased.

If you go to the Zoo, Australia's Wonderland or the Aquarium you can purchase link tickets which include transport and entry to the venue.

Getting through the automatic ticket barriers

To get through these barriers make sure you choose one with a green arrow, not a red cross. Your ticket will have an arrow on it; insert your ticket in the front of the machine, and if it is a single ticket the gates will open allowing you through. If it is a return ticket or a pass, collect it from the top of the machine. Then the gates will open and you can walk through. If you have any problems, see one of the attendants.

The ferries

The ferries are a great way to see the harbour and to get you from one side of the city to the other.

They run from 6.00 am to midnight and travel between Circular Quay and the other harbour areas.

It's easy to ride on a ferry. Just buy a ticket from the wharf, run it through the automatic turnstiles and away you go.

Besides point-to-point services, ferries can give you a tour around the harbour. Find out more from the Ferry Ticket Office which is opposite Wharf 4 at Circular Quay.

Walking

Sydney's tourist areas are relatively close together, making walking a viable option. Wear comfortable shoes.

The traffic lights amuse many tourists as they make a noise to let you know when to cross the road. You'll find out!

Hitting Sydney's tourist spots—a suggestion

The part of Sydney everyone heads to first is Circular Quay, to see the Harbour Bridge and the Opera House.

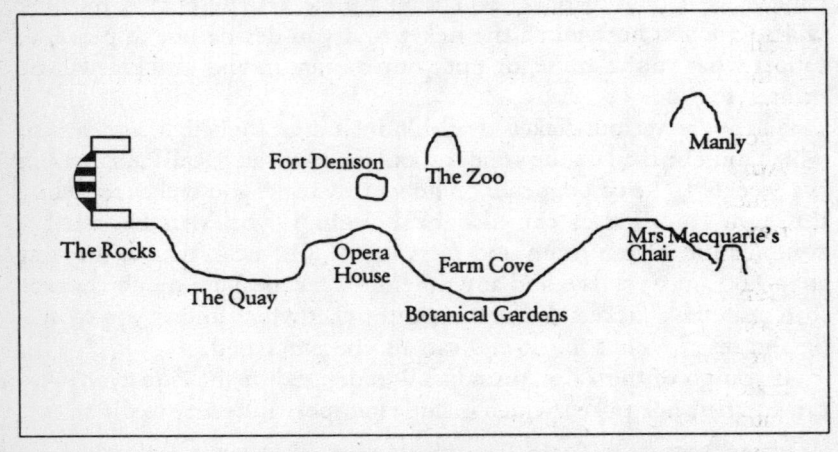

Starting at Circular Quay, follow **Writers' Walk** to Bennelong Point where the **Opera House** is. Here you could take a tour of the various theatres and halls and walk around the unusual building itself.

What is that castle-like building sitting in the middle of the harbour? It is **Fort Denison**, once used as a convict prison.

Leaving the Opera House walk along the foreshore of Farm Cove, which was the original farming ground of the first white settlers and is now the Botanical Gardens, to **Mrs Macquarie's Chair**. There you can sit back and relax just like Mrs Macquarie did in the 1800s, but you will have a view of the Opera House and the Harbour Bridge.

From here walk back through the **Botanical Gardens** to Circular Quay and follow Writers' Walk to **The Rocks**. This is where the original settlement of Sydney began under Captain Arthur Phillip. You can stroll along narrow, cobbled streets and amongst sandstone buildings while browsing through the shops.

From The Rocks you can ascend the pylons of the **Harbour Bridge**. Access is by the pedestrian walk-way off Cumberland Street. You might like to walk the 'Coathanger' or catch a train or bus across and take in the view. I think your feet will be aching by now, I know mine were way back at the Botanical Gardens, so enough sightseeing for today.

Other things to do include:

- Take a ferry from Circular Quay to **Taronga Park Zoo** and get the animals'-eye view of the harbour.
- Take the half-hour ferry ride from Circular Quay to **Manly** and visit the **Oceanarium**, or stroll the esplanade and take in the beachside atmosphere. From Manly wharf catch the **Northern Beaches Explorer** bus which visits **Palm Beach**, where some of the scenes of *Home and Away* are filmed. Or you could walk from the wharf to the **Quarantine Station** at North Head.
- Still on the harbour, you might like to take a morning, afternoon or dinner **cruise**. Boats leave from Circular Quay or further down past the Overseas Terminal.
- Another day, catch the monorail to **Darling Harbour** and visit the **Australian Maritime Museum**, or browse around the shops, have a meal, a bet at the **Casino**; perhaps take a walk through the **Sydney Aquarium**, enjoy the free entertainment or visit an exhibition in one of the exhibition halls. Take in a show at the **Entertainment Centre** or walk through the **Chinese Gardens**.
- Sports enthusiasts might want to visit the **SCG** (Sydney Cricket Ground) and the **Football Stadium**, or get tickets to a sporting match.
- Catch the lift up **Sydney Tower**, Sydney's tallest building, to the observation level for a 360-degree view of the city. Splurge on a meal at one of the revolving restaurants. Choose a clear day or evening to do so.

- Step back to convict times at the **Hyde Park Barracks**.
- Art enthusiasts might want to visit the **Art Gallery** or see some contemporary art at the **Brett Whiteley Studio** in Surry Hills.
- If you are interested in seeing the birthplace of white Australia, you might like to hire a car and visit **Botany Bay** in the southern suburbs.
- Count grains of sand on any number of Sydney's beaches.
- Those of you not staying in **Kings Cross** might want to go and see for yourself what all the fuss is about during the day, or visit it at night.
- Punters might like to spend a day at the races, a night at the trots or dogs.
- If you want to get close to some native fauna you may wish to visit one of the wildlife parks, or wait and see the animals in the wild.
- Take in a free lunchtime concert at **Martin Place** amphitheatre or pay a visit to the **Cenotaph**.
- You could visit the Year 2000 **Olympic site** at Homebush Bay and see how it is shaping up, or shape up yourself in the Olympic pool.

Day and weekend trips from Sydney

To find out more about what to do in New South Wales visit the NSW Tourist Bureau at 19 Castlereagh Street, pick up the brochures, then get going! Some suggestions are:

The **Blue Mountains** are west of Sydney and get their name from the blue haze created by the eucalyptus oil in the air above the gum trees. You can drive up to the mountains or take the scenic rail trip to **Katoomba** and say G'day to the **Three Sisters**. You could ride the **Skyway Cable Car** for a panoramic view of the area. There is a hop-on hop-off **Blue Mountains Explorer** bus which you could take or, as the area is a bushwalker's paradise, you may like to hike along one of the many tracks.

If you like caves then you might want to visit the **Jenolan Caves**. If you are feeling energetic, they are a 42 km bushwalk from Katoomba—or take a tour.

A couple of hours north of Sydney is the **Hunter Valley** region, famous for its wines. You might want to visit some of the wineries and sample a few vintages.

South of Sydney is the oldest national park in Australia: the **Royal National Park** with beautiful beaches and picnic areas.

Further south is **Wollongong**, 'The Gong', with beautiful beaches, and the magnificent **Nan Tien Buddhist Temple**.

Beyond 'The Gong' is **Kiama**, famous for its blowhole. Buy some fish and chips and sit and wait for it to blow, but don't get too close or you might be washed in.

Even further south are the crystal waters of **Jervis Bay**, a place favoured by many dolphins and whales. Just north of Batemans Bay (south of Jervis Bay) is **Pebbly Beach**, where the kangaroos occasionally surf.

Cricket enthusiasts might wish to visit **Bowral**—the childhood home of Sir Don Bradman, 'The Don', and visit his cricket museum.

For those who'd like to see a re-creation of how Sydney was when the white settlers first arrived, you might like to step back in time at **Old Sydney Town**, just north of Sydney.

Further afield in New South Wales

New South Wales is more than just Sydney and its surrounds; there are plenty of other towns to visit. If you have your own car you can explore places at your leisure, but you can take the train or a bus as well.

Countrylink trains service many areas of New South Wales. You could purchase a **NSW Discovery Pass** for travel on trains throughout the state. Trains leave from **Central Station** where there is a major Countrylink Travel Centre so you can find out what is available.

Places you might wish to visit include:

Canberra is the nation's capital and is well worth a few days' visit. There is a hop-on hop-off bus you might like to take as the sights are quite a distance apart, or you could hire a bike. Canberra is built for bike riders with many cycle tracks.

Visit the **new Parliament House**, **old Parliament House**, the **War Memorial**, the **Royal Australian Mint**, the **Botanical Gardens** and the **Lodge**, home of the Prime Minister. View the art at the **National Gallery** or go to the top of the **Telecom Tower** on **Black Mountain** for a view over the city; visit the **Australian Institute of Sport** or take a cruise on **Lake Burley Griffin**.

It is only an hour or so to the **Kosciusko National Park** where many of Australia's ski fields are. During winter you can ski and in the summer you can bushwalk. You could visit the **Snowy Mountains Scheme** which is well-known as an engineering feat.

You could visit **Gundagai** and see the dog sitting on his tuckerbox, and maybe learn the words to *The Road to Gundagai*.

Dubbo offers history in the form of some of Australia's most notorious bushrangers and murderers, and it also has the **Western Plains Zoo** which houses many African animals, as the weather in Dubbo is similar to that of the African savanna lands. The Zoo has several breeding programs including one for the black rhino.

Visit **Broken Hill,** a mining town near the South Australian border.

Many artists live here and capture the colours of the outback on canvas. Maybe you could stay at **Mario's Palace Hotel** where the 'girls' from *Priscilla, Queen of the Desert* stayed. You could also visit the **School of the Air** and the **Royal Flying Doctor Service**.

There is an Australian saying, 'the back of Bourke', meaning the back of nowhere. Maybe you'd like to visit **Bourke**, if only to say you've been there, or to visit the **Gunderbook** Aboriginal art caves.

Sightseeing the rest of Australia

The coach left Alice Springs on time at 8.30 pm but soon the backpacker sitting next to me was enquiring did I know how much longer it was till we'd be there? Her jawed dropped to the floor when I told her we weren't due in Darwin till 3.30 tomorrow afternoon. She looked at her watch and counted around its face. 'But that's another 17 hours!' she exclaimed. All up, the trip from Alice Springs to Darwin took 19 hours.

As I recovered from my trip by the pool, another girl joined me and soon revealed that she had just arrived in Darwin after a 33-hour bus journey from Cairns. And so the stories continue of many travellers who don't realise the distances involved in travelling Australia.

If your aim is really to experience Australia by seeing all there is to see and trying all the activities there are to try, then you really need to spend as long as possible travelling. Three to six months is the norm for working holidaymakers, though it really is up to you. You should take into account actual travelling time to places (and recovery time).

To help you make the most of your trip, I have included a map of major attractions including the activities available there and how long they take. Once you have a rough time-frame you can work out how to get around by linking the available options. Read on.

Holidaying

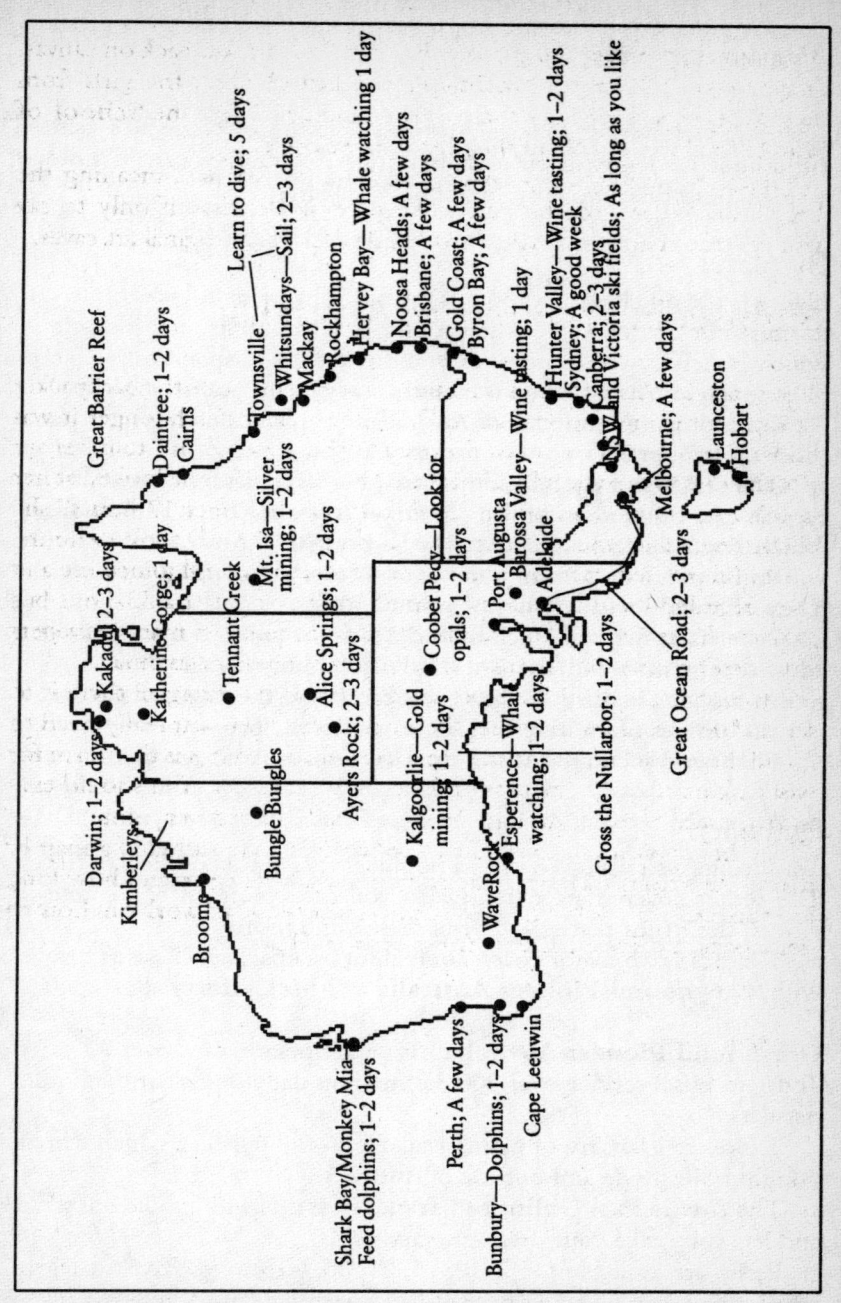

- Great Barrier Reef
- Daintree; 1–2 days
- Cairns
- Learn to dive; 5 days
- Townsville
- Whitsundays—Sail; 2–3 days
- Mackay
- Rockhampton
- Hervey Bay—Whale watching 1 day
- Noosa Heads; A few days
- Brisbane; A few days
- Gold Coast; A few days
- Byron Bay; A few days
- Hunter Valley—Wine tasting; 1–2 days
- Sydney; A good week
- Canberra; 2–3 days
- NSW and Victoria ski fields; As long as you like
- Melbourne; A few days
- Launceston
- Hobart
- Mt. Isa—Silver mining; 1–2 days
- Tennant Creek
- Alice Springs; 2–3 days
- Coober Pedy—Look for opals; 1–2 days
- Port Augusta
- Barossa Valley—Wine tasting; 1–2 days
- Adelaide
- Great Ocean Road; 2–3 days
- Kakadu; 2–3 days
- Katherine Gorge; 1 day
- Darwin; 1–2 days
- Kimberleys
- Broome
- Bungle Bungles
- Ayers Rock; 2–3 days
- Kalgoorlie—Gold mining; 1–2 days
- Esperance—Whale watching; 1–2 days
- Cross the Nullarbor; 1–2 days
- Wave Rock
- Shark Bay/Monkey Mia—Feed dolphins; 1–2 days
- Perth; A few days
- Bunbury—Dolphins; 1–2 days
- Cape Leeuwin

So you've looked at the map and you know what you want to see. Now you need to know how to travel.

115

Travel options

There are various ways to travel Australia including by plane, by coach—either independently or on organised tours, by train, by car, by motor-bike, by push bike and even by yacht.

By plane

Flying is the quickest method to get you from point-to-point but you do miss out on what's between A and B. If you're limited by time—which hopefully you're not—or you don't want to spend many hours or even days on a bus or train then this may be an option for you.

If you didn't enquire about Australian air passes before you arrived there are still several options open to you.

QANTAS and **Ansett** are the two big airlines servicing all major capitals and other areas of the country. They offer **backpacker fares** which might suit you and can only be bought in Australia. At present you must purchase a minimum of 2 sectors and cannot back-track. They offer fares with savings of around 40%.

Other fares available include the 21-day advance purchase, 14-day advance purchase and the 7-day advance purchase, all of which are return flights. The further ahead you can book, the cheaper the flight.

The airlines often have specials, so watch the papers for these.

Flight and accommodation package deals are also available.

By coach

Traversing Australia by coach is a popular way for backpackers to travel. The routes covered are extensive so you can count on being able to visit all the major places you want to see, and more.

There are two major coach companies backpackers choose to travel with, **Greyhound Pioneer Australia** and **McCafferty's**.

Greyhound Pioneer Australia has been operating for over 90 years. Today its buses service over 900 destinations daily on its national route network.

There are a variety of passes available to the traveller which can be bought both inside and outside of Australia.

The **Aussie Pass Unlimited Travel Pass** offers unlimited bus travel and lets you make your own itinerary.

Passes are available for 7, 10, 15, 21, 30, 60 and 90 days' worth of travel which can be taken over non-consecutive days. There is a time-frame to use the ticket but it does allow for plenty of time to stay in places you like. For example, a 7-day pass is valid for 30 days.

At the time of publication a 7-day bus pass cost A$475, a 10-day pass A$610, 15 days A$710, 21 days $A935, 30 days A$1135, 60 days A$1695 and a 90-day pass A$2335. If you hold a YHA, VIP, ISIC or Euro 26 card, concession rates apply. Please note that the prices quoted are in Australian dollars and can change.

Greyound Pioneer also has **Aussie Pass Value Packages** which are set route passes covering the entire Greyhound Pioneer Australia network. For instance if you want to make your way leisurely from Sydney to Cairns or vice versa, you could purchase a **Sunseeker Pass** which allows you to hop on and hop off the bus at various destinations. At the time of publication a Sunseeker Pass cost A$220. Or if you want to visit the outback you could take the **Rock Track** which will get you to Kakadu from Darwin before travelling down to Alice Springs and out to Ayers Rock/Uluru. At the time of publication this pass cost A$275.

To find out more about Greyhound Pioneer passes and their prices pick up a brochure from a travel agency or contact their 24-hour Australia-wide number: 132 030.

Greyhound Pioneer Australia in conjunction with YHA have produced a route map which shows you where all the YHA hostels are. This can help you work out your itinerary.

McCafferty's first bus was run in Toowoomba (west of Brisbane) in April 1940 by Jack McCafferty. Today they operate more than 1000 regular scheduled services every week, covering extensive routes around Australia, which is very pleasing to travellers.

Besides point-to-point travel McCafferty's have 15 passes designed to suit independent travellers' needs. These passes allow you to hop on and hop off the bus at many destinations.

If you want to follow the sun along Australia's east coast you could do so. At the time of publication a **Follow the Sun** pass, valid for three months and departing from Sydney cost A$178.

If you want to travel the red centre you could purchase a **Territory Adventurer**, or if you want to travel the west coast of Australia you could purchase a **West Coast Adventurer**. You could travel all around Australia if you wanted to.

There are concessions for YHA, VIP and ISIC card holders.

To find out more about McCafferty's passes pick up a brochure from a travel agent who deals with bus companies or contact them direct on their Australia-wide number: 131 499

As well as the above two companies, smaller bus companies like **Kirklands** operate between Brisbane, Sydney and Melbourne while **Firefly Express** operates between Sydney, Melbourne and Adelaide. Check them out.

If you are taking a long bus trip here are some suggestions to make that trip even better.

It can get cold on the bus so wear something warm or take a blanket or towel to throw over yourself. Also take a pillow or something to lean on. If you get a window seat you can lean against the window but I have found that it vibrates, so having something to absorb the quivering will help you get some sleep.

If possible, request a seat near the front of the bus so you don't get the smells from the chemical toilet. Also, people often slam the door even though they are asked not to. Hopefully you'll have a seat on the left-hand side of the bus so you don't get the headlights from other traffic in your eyes. Save some money and take your own snacks and drinks for the bus trip. Stopping at roadhouses can prove costly and the food is mostly fast food.

Get out and stretch your legs when the bus stops. Just like flying, with lack of exercise your feet can swell—buslag.

People often take night drives to save on accommodation but if you haven't slept properly you will alight tired and lacklustre and in need of a rest before going into tourist mode. Maybe you can travel during the day, and see the landscape unfold.

To tour or not to tour—this is the question
As well as the bus passes mentioned above there are also bus tours and independent bus travel. The difference between the latter two being: on bus tours you are ferried from sight to sight and have your accommodation and most meals included, whereas independent bus travel is aimed more at those who still want to see the sights but are given the opportunity to experience out-of-the-way places and try many activities. They allow you more freedom and if you like a place you can stay and pick up another of the company buses later on.

There is nothing wrong with either option; it just depends on what you want. Pick up brochures from travel agencies for **Contiki** and **Connections** which have tours all over Australia and cater for the 18–35-year-olds.

Information on more independent bus trips like **Straycat**, **Wayward Bus**, **Oz Experience**, **Pioneering Spirit** or **Andos Outback Experience** can be found at specialist backpacker travel agencies, YHA, STA and some hostels (see where 'to organise your travel' further on in this section).

By train
Train routes aren't as extensive as the bus routes but there are still some wonderful trips to take.

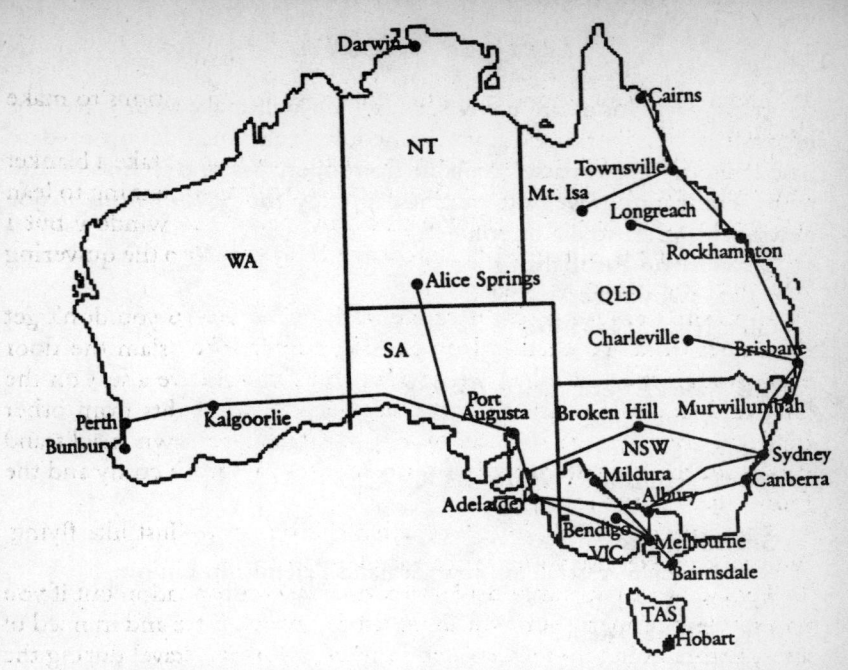

The most well-known train route is that of the **Indian Pacific** which takes three days to travel between Sydney and Perth. There is also the **Ghan** which runs between Adelaide and Alice Springs.

Many holidaymakers like train travel, as you can get up and move around or have a bite to eat in the buffet car or a drink at the bar. If you want a bed you can pay a little extra for a sleeper.

Passes available include the **Austrail Flexipass** and the **Austrailpass**. Both passes are available for use on the trains over a certain number of days. Ask your travel agent for a brochure about the passes.

The different states also have a variety of passes available. You could travel the east coast on the **East Coast Discovery Pass**. In New South Wales there is the **NSW Discovery Pass**, in Queensland the **Sunshine Rail Pass**, in Victoria the **Victoria Pass** and in Western Australia there are the **Westrail Premier Discovery Pass** and **Western Southern Discovery Pass**.

Ask for a brochure about the passes and read up on them before you purchase.

Travel Times Australia is the bible for independent travellers. It answers that major question poised on the lips; what time does the train, bus or ferry leave?

As Australia does not have one major operator to provide a timetable of services, Traveltime Publishing has put together a guide listing over 300 of the latest timetables and covering over 250 operators of trains, coaches and ferries throughout Australia. They are arranged so that all the transport options are easily seen, which will make your travelling life easier when working out your schedule. It also includes up-to-date base fares, the major passes available from operators, and it shows route maps. For happy travelling, purchase a copy for A$7.95 from major newsagents in Australia or contact:

Traveltime Publishing
3 Goodwin Street
Glen Iris VIC 3146

UK Sales Agent (price £7.95):
4 Haydock Close
Kimberley
Nottinghamshire NG16 2TX

Scandinavia:
Scandinavian Australian New Zealand Friendship Union
Norregade 51
DK-7500 Hostebro
Denmark

USA (price US$11.50):
World Rail Travel Specialists
PO Box 732, East Moriches
New York 11940-0732

To **organise your travel** the places which specialise in backpacking and budget travel within Australia follow. They are in alphabetical order and not in order of preference.

Backpackers Travel Centre has its nerve centre near Sydney's Bondi beach.

Sydney
Shop 4, Bronka Arcade
Oxford Street Mall
Bondi Junction NSW 2022
Tel (02) 369 1331

Other outlets include:

Sydney office
Shop 33, Pitt Street Mall Level
Imperial Arcade
Sydney NSW 2000
Tel: (02) 231 3699

Brisbane office
Room 12, Balcony Level
Brisbane Arcade
Queen Street Mall
Brisbane QLD 400
Tel (07) 3221 2225

Melbourne office
Shop 19, Centre Place
258 Flinders Lane
Melbourne VIC 3000
Tel (03) 9654 8477

Eden Travel
Shop 6, Corner Orwell and Springfield Avenue
Potts Point NSW 2011
Tel: (02) 368 1174

Let's Travel Australia
165 Victoria Street
Kings Cross NSW 2011
Tel: (02) 358 2295

Traveller's Contact Point
Level 7, 428 George Street
Sydney NSW 2000
Tel (02) 221 8744

STA have travel offices all over Australia.

YHA Travel Centres (there is one in all major capitals) plus some YHA hostels.

Most hostels carry brochures and can book your trips for you or advise you where else you can go for bookings.

By car/van
Flexibility is the name of the game when you travel by car. You can go where you want, when you want and include out-of-the-way places that coach and train travellers will miss.

There are various ways to get your hands on the wheel of a car—all legal of course! You could rent a car or campervan, relocate a car or campervan, buy your own vehicle or share a lift.

Renting and relocating a car/van
There are national car rental companies which rent various types of cars. This option can work out to be quite expensive if you don't have a full car-load of people. If you are going to hire a car or van shop around for the best rates. Some rental companies give special discounts to those holding YHA membership cards and some of them work in conjunction with the airlines—can you use those accumulated air miles?

One-way rentals can be obtained through the national car companies, and they often need these cars relocated to their home office so ask them about this.

Besides the major national companies you will often find local car rental companies where you can rent a car for a day or two.

Backpackers often rent campervans to take into the outback. These homes-on-wheels often require drivers to relocate them. Contact:

Brits: Australia Rentals and Tours

This is the largest leisure vehicle rental company in Australia with an extensive range of motorhomes, campervans and four-wheel drives (including bushcampers).

They often require relocation drivers between their branches in Sydney, Brisbane, Cairns, Darwin, Perth, Alice Springs, Adelaide and Melbourne.

You need to be over 23 years of age and have a current Australian, overseas or international driver's licence.

It costs A$10 a day plus petrol. Your accommodation and living equipment travels with you.

A small bond of A$500 is required and refunded when the vehicle is delivered to its allocated destination, undamaged with the interior clean and fuel tank full.

Tel: (07) 3262 8822 (Relocations)
Free call: 1800 331 454 (Central Reservations)

Oz Rentals

Besides renting campervans and four-wheel drives, they require relocation drivers.

They have an Australia-wide network allowing the pick-up/drop-off of vehicles from Adelaide, Alice Springs, Ayers Rock/Uluru, Brisbane, Broome, Cairns, Darwin, Perth, Sydney, Townsville and their head office in Melbourne. So if you are looking for a way to tour Australia without the worry of buying a vehicle or missing that bus or train, relocation is an option you could consider. In a way it is like renting a vehicle for a far cheaper price as you pay just A$2 per day plus fuel costs. Discounted hire rates are also available at various times throughout the year.

A bond of A$1000 is required which will be returned when the vehicle arrives at the designated destination in the pre-arranged timeframe and is clean with a full tank of petrol. Vehicles are only allowed to be driven on sealed roads and night driving is not allowed while you're on relocations and this will aid in the return of your A$1000.

Tel: (03) 9874 5633

Buying a car/van is an option many travellers choose. One drawback is the up-front funding required to purchase a vehicle but hey, you will be selling it at the end of your journey anyway, unless you intend folding it up and squeezing it into the little air pocket in your backpack that is! It is wise if a few of you can pool your resources to buy your car/van.

So how much do you need to buy a car? Of course prices will differ, but budget to spend up to A$5,000. Holy @%*£! you've just yelled! This is really at the top end of the backpacker spending scale. I've seen many an advertisement on hostel noticeboards and the asking prices vary greatly; some are as low as A$750.

Even though price is a major concern, what you really need is a guarantee that the vehicle you purchase will complete the travelling you want to do without any hassles. Hassles meaning having to fork out money to have a major part replaced.

When looking at vehicles, you need to consider where your travels will take you and how many people will be going with you.

Six-cylinder cars are highly recommended as their engines and cooling systems are bigger, and cope better in the hot weather of Far North Queensland and the Northern Territory. They also have more room.

Station wagons are a good choice as you can sleep in the back. A popular car is the Ford Falcon station wagon.

Many travellers purchase combi vans because they provide accommodation but they do tend to suffer in the heat as they are air-cooled. In a hot area, hot air will be cooling the engine.

So where can you buy a car? Cars can be bought privately or through car dealerships.

Bought privately

So you've found the car you want to buy, but before you hand over any money you need to do the following things:

Firstly see a valid **Pink Slip** (this can be called by a different name in each state), which is not more than one month old and states that the car is roadworthy. A **Black Slip** will indicate what is wrong with the car. Even after seeing this you might want to have the car checked over by a mechanic or a motoring organisation. Motoring organisations do require you to be a member. Did you bring your CMC with you?

The main question you need answered is, Will the car complete the travelling I want to do?

Also contact the **Registry of Encumbered Vehicles** (in Sydney, (02) 600 0022) to find out if there is any money owing on the car, like a loan or traffic fines. If there is, and you buy the car, you are liable.

Once these two things are done, check that the person selling the car is the person named on the registration papers. If they are, then purchase the car. I'd be suspicious about someone selling the car for someone who has left the country.

Cars are registered once a year (again, registration laws depend on which state you are in), so when you're buying a car see how much registration is left. When the registration is still valid, the car only needs to have the registration owner changed from old to new. This is done by having the registered owner sign the back of the registration paper which you then take, along with the pink slip, to a motor registry to have your details inserted.

Insurance covering any people hurt in an accident is compulsory and usually included in your registration (it is done this way in New South Wales and is referred to as a **Green Slip**).

Third Party Property insurance to cover any damage to vehicles should be taken out, but unfortunately no insurance company will insure someone from overseas. Not to worry as car dealers can arrange this for you, or contact the Kings Cross Car Market which has a specific policy for overseas residents. At the time of publication this cost A$180 for three months and can be arranged 24-hours a day, seven days a week on Freecall 1800 801 188. Or you could fax them (see their details following).

Private sales are advertised on hostel noticeboards and in the newspapers. Saturday's papers are particularly good, as is the weekly *Trading Post* available at newsagents.

Bought through a car dealer

Buying a car through a dealer is an easier process as dealers are responsible for having their cars roadworthy and free of any encumbrances. They can also advise on vehicle registration and insurance.

The following Sydney car dealers specialise in cars/vans for backpackers:

Auto Becker has been selling cars to backpackers for over 10 years. They have a wide variety available including station wagons, campervans, and four-wheel drives. They can advise you on insurance and registration, etc. You may contact them before you arrive, advising them of your arrival date so Auto Becker can keep a look-out for a suitable car.

Auto Becker
16–20 Oxford Street
Paddington NSW 2021
Tel: (02) 360 7211
Fax: (02) 337 4202
Mobile: 018 407 047
(Paddington is Sydney suburb near Kings Cross.)

Another dealership selling cars to travellers is:
Traveller's Auto Barn
177 William Street
Kings Cross 2011
Tel: (02) 360 1500
Fax: (02) 360 1977

Some car dealers include a guaranteed buy-back scheme so that after your travels are completed they will buy the car back from you. The good thing about this is that you know you have a buyer for the vehicle. At the time of purchase discuss the terms of a buy-back scheme with them. It is usually around 50% which means if you bought a car for A$4000 and drove it for 3 months you would receive A$2000 back. But confirm the details with the dealer.

If you are going to sell the vehicle privately, make sure you allow yourself time to sell it.

If you sell/buy a car in a different state from where the car is registered, check if the registration can be transferred by mail.

A place to privately buy and sell a car is:

The Kings Cross Car Market which is dedicated to international car travellers. Here you can meet and buy/sell cars/campervans from/to fellow travellers. You may only lose about 10–20% on the price you paid for the vehicle. You may even pick up some camping gear. Those who run the market are also available to advise you on registration and insurance.

No commission is charged for selling your car here but a A$5 fee per day (A$35 for the week) is required to park and sell the car there.

The market is undercover and has phones, hot water, electricity, toilets, a fridge, lounge, TV, etc. for your convenience while you're waiting to sell your vehicle. There is also a free barbecue every Thursday for sellers/buyers.

The Kings Cross Car Market has a help hot-line (see number below) open seven days a week from 9 am to 6 pm to advise the caller on buying, selling, transferring, renewing registration, etc. even if you aren't buying/didn't buy there.

The Kings Cross Car Market
Cnr Ward Ave & Elizabeth Bay Road
Kings Cross NSW 2011
Tel: (02) 358 5000
Fax: (02) 358 5102
Help Hot-Line 1 902 263 180 (A$2 per minute from anywhere in Australia).

Flemington Car Market has on average around 200 cars to be sold by private Sydney sellers every Sunday. Each vehicle on display must have current registration papers, pink slip and owner identification. Mechanical inspections can be done at the market and you could drive away with a car.

To get to Flemington, take the train to Flemington station.

Sharing a lift is an option for travellers. There are people out there who have bought a car but don't have the bodies to fill it, so they advertise for travel companions.

Most lifts are advertised on hostel noticeboards and can read something like 'person required to make up 4th on a ramble up east coast. Leaving Sydney Monday to be in Byron Bay by Friday. Contact.....'. So if you're either looking for or offering a lift, place your ads on the hostel noticeboards or try:

Australian Car-Pooling Agency (ACPA) operates throughout Australia, offering interstate car-pooling and car-pooling to work. The service is entirely free for people offering lifts. If you need a lift, registration itself is free; when ACPA finds you a lift, a A$10 service fee is applicable. The petrol bill for the trip is shared equally.

Most interstate lifts offered or needed are currently between the bigger cities and along the coast up to Cairns. Registering about five days before your trip gives you a much better chance.

Car-pooling can also be used to travel short distances at regular intervals, mainly to and from work every day. This service is at the moment limited to the greater metropolitan areas of Sydney, Melbourne and Brisbane. Registration is free and can be in three categories: passenger, driver or both possible. The current service fee for successful matching is A$30 per person. It is payable only once and covers the actual matching plus some guidance on how to get the most out of the arrangement.

Brisbane: (07) 3229 4777
Melbourne: (03) 9826 3266
Sydney: (02) 9411 6786

From any other place in Australia (Perth, Adelaide, etc.) the Sydney number should be called.

Cycling

Australia is becoming more of a cycle-friendly place, with many roads now providing cycle lanes, though in the cities these aren't really respected as they often get in the way of intolerant motorists.

Realistically, a bike will be all right for transport around the city or for making short trips, but you'll need a lot of time if you're travelling around Australia, time which many working holidaymakers don't have.

If you do get a bike, it is compulsory to wear a helmet. Make sure you take plenty of water, spares and a tool kit. Wear brightly-coloured clothes, and have lights and things that sparkle on the bike so you will stand out.

Hitching

Since the grisly discovery of seven backpacker bodies in the Belanglo State Forest in the Southern Highlands of New South Wales, it is strongly recommended that you do not hitchhike—though people still do.

If you do hitch, have a sign to say where you are going. Be selective with lifts and advise someone (the hostel, a friend) where you are going and your planned arrival time, so if you don't arrive they can alert police.

I've heard that if you enquire at the roadhouses where the truckies stop, you may get a lift with a truckie. They don't often stop on the road unless it is flat, as they lose their revs.

Yacht crewing

This is a possibility for those who want to get off the land and hitch a ride up the east coast. Your best bet is to go to the docks and ask around, enquire in the yacht clubs or leave a notice on the club noticeboards.

You will mostly have to contribute towards food supplies and the running of the boat but hey, what a way to travel! Hopefully, it will be smooth sailing.

There are not always facilities for yachts to pull into coastal towns, so ask yachting enthusiasts which places are popular.

From Hobart, the boats return up north after the Sydney to Hobart race which leaves Sydney on Boxing Day. Other coastal destinations where you might pick up a lift are Nelson Bay, Coffs Harbour, Yamba, Ballina, Brisbane, the Whitsundays and Cairns.

Most boats stay up north for the winter months, then head south for the summer to avoid the cyclone season.

Lifts can be caught to Darwin as many go there for the Darwin to Ambon (located in Indonesia) race in July. During summer a lot of the boats are land-locked because of the cyclones.

Seeing the rest of Australia

This sightseeing section will not tell you the ins and outs of towns and cities in Australia. If you want to know the population of each town, the annual rainfall, where the public toilets are, how many pubs exist, where someone famous sat on a bench to watch the world go by, there are plenty of guides on the market for that. So what does this section cover then? It suggests some possible routes to make the most of your travels.

Suggested routes

The East Coast—Sydney to Cairns

The east coast stretches, well, along all of the east coast of Australia! Most travellers go from Sydney to Cairns, or Cairns to Sydney. For the sake of this guide we will go Sydney to Cairns. If you are travelling Cairns to Sydney, you'll have to read backwards!

Travelling up (or down) the east coast is a track well worn by travellers. Those with cars will have more opportunity to get off this track and see out-of-the-way things. There are many scenic tourist drives, pristine beaches, rainforests and historic sites, and if something catches your eye you can take off and have a look.

Ways to do this route include using the hop-on hop-off bus passes of Greyhound Pioneer or McCafferty's. You could take a tour with Contiki, Connection or a more adventurous trip with Oz Experience, Surfaris, Andos Outback Experience, etc.

Leaving Sydney, you will travel north along the Pacific Highway. Your first stop could be at **Gosford** on the Central Coast. There are some beautiful beaches here; it could be a great weekend escape from Sydney.

Newcastle is the second largest city in New South Wales. It is an industrial town with the Newcastle Steel Works. There are some beautiful beaches here. You could visit the Hunter Valley, a major wine producing area, and taste a few varieties.

From Newcastle you could head to **Nelson Bay** and Port Stephens.

Port Stephens is off the main highway but this huge port houses many bays and beaches. Another great de-stressing area. If you have your own transport you could travel from Nelson Bay at the south end of the port around to the Great Lakes at the north. There you'll find the Myall Lakes National Park where you might see kangaroos and koalas in their natural habitat.

Forster is another place Sydneysiders go for a weekend.

Port Macquarie is another place to lie on a beach and relax for a while.

Coffs Harbour is home to the Big Banana which you might want to have your photo taken in front of. Come on, be a tourist.

Many stop at **Nimbin**, hippy capital of Australia.

The coast road from **Ballina** to **Byron Bay** is spectacular. At Byron, as it's affectionately called, you could do the Cape Byron walk which will take you the lighthouse where you could dolphin and whale watch. Also take in the fact that you are standing on the most eastern point of Australia. Another photo opportunity.

You might want to spend a few days in Byron lazing on the beach, learning to surf or relaxing in one of the cafes. The place is very laid back and alternative and is home to ferals and hippies who have chosen to leave the rat race.

From Byron you may like to stop at **Murwillumbah** and take a trip to **Mount Warning** which is where the first rays of sunlight touch Australia each day.

The **Gold Coast** isn't everyone's cup of tea. The strip running for 42 km from Tweed Heads up to Southport covers some beautiful beaches but it is also very commercial with many highrise apartments. If ever you wanted to splurge out and stay away from a hostel this is a place to do it because there is so much accommodation catering for every budget.

It is home to three theme parks, Movie World, Dreamworld and Seaworld. There is also Wet 'n' Wild water park.

You might want to try your luck at Jupiter's Casino.

There are many car rental companies on the Gold Coast renting vehicles for a day. You might wish to do this and travel west to Tamborine Mountain, walk through the rainforest and possibly see platypus in the creeks. You could also explore the Tweed Valley.

You could take a cruise to North or South Stradbroke Islands.

For those not wanting to spend all their time on a beach, take the New England Highway route and travel via Tamworth, home of Australian country music. Keep following the road to Tenterfield, birthplace of Peter Allen, and pop in to the saddler's shop on the High Street before heading to Brisbane.

Brisbane is the capital of Queensland. You may want to spend a few days here seeing the sights of this city. If you are looking for accommodation enquire at the Roma Street Transit Centre where there is an accommodation desk.

You might wish to take the hop-on hop-off City Sights tour to hear some history of Brisbane, and see the major sights including the Cultural Centre at Southbank where Expo 88 was staged.

You may wish to go to Mt Coot-tha for a panoramic view over the city.

Plane fanciers might wish to visit the *Southern Cross*, Charles Kingsford-Smith's plane, at Brisbane Airport.

Rum fanciers may wish to tour the Beenleigh Rum Distillery.

Dolphin lovers could visit Tangalooma on Moreton Bay Island and feed the dolphins which come there nightly.

Take a cruise to Stradbroke Island if you haven't already done so from the Gold Coast.

For an outback Aussie experience you may wish to see the sheep shearing at the Australian Woolshed.

Take a walk through the Queen Street Mall, the heart of the city, and shop till you drop or relax with a coffee.

Try your luck at Conrad Treasury Casino.

Maybe take a river cruise along the Brisbane River.

Beer enthusiasts may wish to tour the XXXX Brewery.

Leaving Brisbane, those with cars may wish to take a scenic drive through pineapple country and have a photo stop at the Big Pineapple on their way via the now extinct volcanoes of the Glasshouse Mountains. Or travel along the beautiful beaches of the Sunshine Coast which is less commercial than the Gold Coast. At the northern end of the Sunshine Coast is subtropical **Noosa Heads,** the Riviera of the Sunshine Coast and a popular spot to stop. You can lie on a beach, try some water sports or walk through Noosa National Park taking in the native flora and fauna.

Next stop could be **Fraser Island**, the largest sand island in the world with a 123 km stretch of sand. It is a World Heritage-listed area and is a nature lover's paradise. Four-wheel drives are the only vehicles allowed on the island. They can be easily rented if you want to explore the island yourself, or you could take one of the available tours. These include day tours for about $60 or camping tours of 2–3 days' duration for $140-200, and are the best way to experience the island. The longer the stay the better.

Hervey Bay is protected by Fraser Island. Most people come here to lie on a beach or catch a boat from Urangan Harbour to go whale watching in the bay.

The whale watching season is from July to October. There are many boats able to take you out to Platypus Bay near the tip of Fraser Island where the whales like to put on displays of breaching and tail and fin slapping. Hopefully they might be so interested in the boat they will come up for a closer look.

Half day and full day tours are offered on various sized boats. Half day tours are the same price as full day tours. The full day tours include lunch.

As it can be rough out there, those who get sea-sick easily but still want to go, might be better off on a half day tour. Hopefully it will be calm but you can't predict the weather.

Don't forget to wear suntan lotion, sunglasses, a hat and maybe take a jumper to keep out the wind. Don't forget the camera.

If you didn't organise a trip out to Fraser Island earlier, one can be arranged from Hervey Bay.

Bundaberg could be your next port of call. This is sugarcane country and home of Bundaberg Rum (Bundy Rum). You might wish to visit the Bundaberg Rum Distillery. Plenty of year-round agricultural work is offered here for those needing to top up their funds. Ask at the hostels.

Lady Musgrave and **Lady Elliot Islands** are accessed from Bundaberg and are good places to swim, fish and dive.

Gladstone is another stop you could make if you want to spend some time on Lady Musgrave or **Heron Islands**.

Rockhampton is the beef capital of Australia. You might wish to visit the **Capricorn Caverns**, with 16 caverns to explore, or the crocodile farm. You could also head out to **Yeppoon** which is the step-off point for those wishing to visit **Great Keppel Island**.

This is also where the **Great Barrier Reef** begins.

It is a long drive to **Mackay**, the stop-off point for **Lindeman** and **Brampton Islands**. Or you could keep on going to **Airlie Beach** which is the gateway to the **Whitsunday Islands**. There are over 70 islands in this group with resorts located only on **Lindeman, Daydream, North Molle, South Molle, Hayman, Hook, Long,** and **Hamilton Islands**.

The resorts offer standby rates if you feel like experiencing a little luxury. Stays can only be booked a couple of days in advance. Ask at one of the many tourist shops along the main strip.

Relaxing here for a few days is well worth your while. You might wish to learn to dive or take a sailing trip around the islands.

There are many boats cruising the islands, from smaller party boats to larger, more luxurious and quieter boats. Most vessels will drop anchor for you to swim and snorkel. Some may even have barbecues on a deserted beach.

Most hostels promote the smaller party boats. If that's what you're after then go for it, if not try and spend a little extra to get what you want. Prices range from around A$230 to A$280 for two or three days' cruising. Where you go depends on the weather.

For those looking for work you might obtain a hospitality position at one of the resorts.

On to **Townsville** which is the third largest city in Queensland. This is the step-off point for those going to **Magnetic Island**. This island is often referred to as the koala capital of Australia as there are thousands of koalas roaming the island. It is also the sunniest spot on the coast with an average of 320 fine days a year.

Day trips to the reef are popular. So is learning to dive. Once you learn you might wish to try Australia's best dive and the sixth best in the world (though some divers will dispute this fact), the **Yongala Wreck**.

Townsville is home to an army base and **James Cook University**, and is the financial capital of North Queensland. You may wish to try your luck at the Sheraton Breakwater Casino.

You might like to walk through the aquarium or go to the top of **Castle Hill** for a panoramic view of the city and the islands beyond.

Many travellers stop at **Cardwell**, the starting point for trips to **Hinchinbrook Island**, the world's largest island national park.

When it's raining in Cairns, many people head for **Mission Beach**, a good place to lie on the sand, or catch the boat to **Dunk Island** where you might see the Ulysses butterfly.

Before reaching Cairns those with a car might wish to visit the **Boulder National Park**. You could walk the rainforest circuit and see the boulders. Be careful when you're walking as there have been many deaths along this path.

Cairns is where the rainforest meets the reef. Like the Gold Coast there is plenty of accommodation to suit all budgets, so if you want that something extra a hostel can't give you, you may wish to upgrade.

Cairns is also a popular place to learn to dive. You'll need five days which covers two days of theory, a day in the pool and two days of diving. You will need to pass a medical to Australian Standard 4005.1 to dive. People with asthma and sinus problems might be excluded from diving as the pressure of being underwater can exacerbate these problems. Don't be too worried if you find your mask has blood in it, as it's quite common for new divers to experience nose bleeds on their first dive due to the water pressure.

Budget around A$450–500 for a course, which covers meals, accommodation on the boat and the use of equipment. Once you've learned, or if you are already an experienced diver, you may wish to undertake other dives along the Great Barrier Reef including a popular spot, the **Cod Hole**.

From Cairns many tours can be undertaken, like a one or two-day tour to **Cape Tribulation**, taking in the magnificent World Heritage-listed **Daintree Rainforest**.

Cairns, like the Gold Coast, has many local car rental operators. You could drive up the mountains to **Kuranda** taking in the **Crater Lakes**, the **Barron Falls** and the **Curtain Fig Tree**. Or take the scenic railway which winds its way up the mountains offering some wonderful views. You could also take the **Skyrail Cableway** to Kuranda.

Walk the esplanade, go shopping or take a sail in Cairns harbour and Everglades to spot estuarine crocodiles, or visit a crocodile farm. Maybe you'd like to go game fishing or take the **Cairns Explorer** hop-on hop-off bus.

You could take a tour hosted by a local Aborigine to learn about the culture of the Aborigines in this area. You might want to try bungee jumping.

You could leave the tropical far north and head in to the **Gulf Savannah** for a trip to the **Undarra Lave Caves**, which are the longest in the world and stretch for some 16 km. On the way you could have a drink at the highest pub in Queensland, in the town of **Tully**. Take note of the signs advising of various battalions which were stationed in the area during WWII.

Cairns is usually the end of this route. A four-wheel drive is necessary to go further. There are tours to take you through to the Cape which can be booked in Cairns.

To/from the outback

To or from the outback (Townsville to Three Ways) is a long way. In fact it is about 2000 km, or a good 25 hours on a bus along the Flinders and Barkly Highways.

Three Ways is so named because there are only three ways to go—to Townsville, to Darwin or to Alice Springs.

Many who drive or bus the trip between Townsville and Three Ways stop at **Mt Isa** which is roughly half-way. Mt Isa has the largest silver mine in Australia. You might want to stop in **Cloncurry** (before or after Mt Isa, depending on which way you are going) where the **Royal Flying Doctor Service** was established in 1928.

If you don't want to drive or bus this distance, you could always use that air pass and fly from Townsville or Cairns to Darwin or Alice Springs—a three or four hour flight.

The outback—down/up the middle

The Stuart Highway runs through the middle of the country from Darwin in the Northern Territory to Port Augusta in South Australia, and links the major attractions.

If you ever ask a Northern Territorian how long it will take to get to a place don't be surprised if they reply 'it should take you a six pack'. The joke is, you never worry about actual distance as it doesn't mean much, it's how many beers you can consume along the way that matters. Strict drinking laws have changed this.

There are long distances involved in driving along this route. Many holidaymakers hire or relocate campervans (see 'Renting and relocating a car/van' in this section) or make use of a Greyhound or McCafferty's bus pass. Tours to major sights can be arranged from the larger centres. From Darwin there are two and three-day tours into **Kakadu**, and from Alice Springs there are two and three-day tours to **Ayers Rock/ Uluru**. Some take the Ghan from Alice to Adelaide and vice versa. There are longer tours which cover all the major sights and include meals and accommodation. These can be booked in either Darwin or Adelaide.

Beginning in Darwin
Darwin is a very compact city and easy to get around, though you may wish to take the hop-on hop-off **Tour Tub** which will take you to the major sights of the city.

Places to visit include the **East Point Military Museum and Reserve** overlooking Darwin harbour, which is where Australia defended its shores from the Japanese during WWII. You may wish to visit **Fanny Bay Gaol** and take a cruise to see the jumping crocodiles. Visit the **Cyclone Tracy** exhibit at the museum and see what Darwin looked like before the city was devastated by the cyclone in 1974.

Everyone goes to the **Mindil Beach Market** to buy some bargains, or to sit on the beach and watch the sunset. The best view of the tropical sunsets is along the harbour foreshores. The sunsets are renowned for their beauty due to Darwin's latitude and longitude and the smog and smoke produced by controlled burns. You may wish to have a flutter at the **Casino**. You could take an organised trip to visit the Tiwi people on **Tiwi Island** off the coast of Darwin. Try some barramundi, either fishing for it, or just eating it.

There aren't many places to swim in Darwin due to the stingers in the water, so stay at a place with a pool.

From Darwin, you must experience **Kakadu**. A good way to do this is by organised tour where you will visit the wetlands, see the crocodiles and other wildlife in their natural environment and gain a knowledge of Aboriginal people through their rock paintings and Dreamtime. You could swim in freshwater billabongs and see beautiful sunsets. Make sure you adhere to the warnings regarding crocodiles.

The first major stop south is **Katherine** to visit the gorge. From Katherine you can take the Victoria Highway to Western Australia.

Next stop, **Mataranka** for a swim in the natural springs.

There are various places to visit along the way, like Three Ways, **Daly Waters**, **Tennant Creek**, **Barrow Creek** and **Ti Tree**. These settlements are there to service the road and some of them are no more than a pub and a road house.

The **Devil's Marbles** near Tennant Creek are large boulders on either side of the road.

Alice Springs is worth a few days' visit. You can walk around town taking in the Aboriginal culture, possibly walk to the top of **Anzac Hill** for a view over the city or walk the 4 km to the **Old Telegraph**

Station where the original springs are. Maybe have a camel ride or go to the camel races.

Not feeling energetic? Then take the hop-on hop-off **Alice Wanderer**. You might wish to take a day trip to explore **Simpson's Gap, Standley Chasm** and the **twin ghost gums**.

The best way to experience **Ayers Rock/Uluru** and its surrounding area is to spend a few days there. Tours can be arranged from Alice Springs which include accommodation—camping is the cheapest—meals and all of your transport. Most tours include watching the monolith change colours at sunset and sunrise, time to climb (though the original land owners prefer you don't do this as the rock is sacred), tour the base by bus or walk the 9 km trip to see Aboriginal paintings and learn about their Dreamtime. You might want to take a flight over 'The Rock', as it is called.

'The Rock' is rather steep to climb. There is a chain for the initial part and after that it does flatten out, but there are still sections you might need a run-up to get over. Try not to take too much with you as it can get in the way. Take a camera and a water bottle in your backpack.

Also visit the **Olgas** and **King's Canyon**.

Tours which include all transport, meals and sights cost around A$200 for two days and around A$275 for three days. There are standby rates, so look out for the brochures. The longer you spend in the area, the more you see and the longer you have to experience it.

Most of the tours end back at Alice Springs, so where do you go from there? Some catch the Ghan to Adelaide, others fly out and most continue on a bus tour or independently.

Coober Pedy is usually the next stop, where the homes are built underground because of the heat. Coober Pedy is the opal capital of Australia where you can fossick for opals yourself.

From here, it's down to **Port Augusta** and on to Adelaide.

From Adelaide many turn left and take the Great Ocean Road to Melbourne, then finish their circle in Sydney. Or turn right and head across the Nullabor to Perth. These are included in 'Across the bottom'.

Across the bottom—Sydney to Perth and vice versa

Ways across the bottom include taking a three-day trip aboard the **Indian Express**, using a bus pass or tour.

There are various highways leading out of Sydney to take you down south. You can stay on the coastal Prince's Highway and stop at popular beach places like **Ulladulla, Batemans Bay, Narooma, Bega, Merimbula** and **Eden** before crossing the border into Victoria to travel along the **Wilderness Coast**.

If you don't want to stick to the coast then head inland to **Canberra**, the nation's capital. From here you can head to **Albury-Wodonga**, then through historic bushranger country to **Melbourne**.

If you are unsure whether or not to get off the bus or train in these places, take a trip on the independent **Straycat** bus service which has two routes to take you from Sydney to Melbourne. One takes two days along the coast from Sydney to Melbourne, and the other takes three days through the high country. Check them out.

Melbourne is the capital of Victoria and worth a few days' visit.

There are various ways to see Melbourne. You can walk to many of the sights, take an organised tour, take a hop-on hop-off double decker **City Explorer** or **City Wanderer** bus tour taking in all the sights, or catch the free burgundy and gold **Circle Tram**.

Sport enthusiasts might want to tour the **MCG** (Melbourne Cricket Ground) to see the change rooms, the **Australian Gallery of Sport**, the long room and members' areas. You could peruse the cricket and AFL memorabilia and sit in the awesome **Great Southern Stand** which holds the capacity of the entire SCG. Or experience a game of AFL or cricket at the ground. From the cricket ground you could visit the **National Tennis Centre** where the Australian Open Tennis Championships are held every January.

On the way to or from the sporting area, walk through **Fitzroy Gardens** to see the **Fairy Tree** and **Captain Cook's Cottage**.

You might want to spend a night at the theatre, dine in **Lygon Street** or **Chinatown**, or go to **Phillip Island** to watch the fairy penguin parade.

You could pick up some bargains at the **Queen Victoria Market** or shop till you drop at **Melbourne Central** or **Swanston Walk**.

Maybe take in a bird's-eye view of Melbourne from the **Rialto Observation Deck**. Go for a walk through the cultural area of **Southgate** or take a cruise along the **Yarra River**.

Walk through the nineteenth century **Old Melbourne Gaol** and see the suit of armour worn by Australia's most famous bushranger, Ned Kelly. Walk in the cell where he was held captive until he was hung from the rafters in the gaol. You can also view the death masks of some gruesome Australian criminals.

See the animals at the **Melbourne Zoo** or venture out to the wildlife park. Take a tram to the **Shrine of Remembrance** and climb the stairs for a view over the city. Visit the **National Gallery** or have a flutter at the **Crown Casino**. *Neighbours* fans can go in search of **Ramsay Street**.

There are many parks and gardens to appreciate, including the **Botanical Gardens**.

Catch a tram to **St Kilda** for some seaside dining and take a walk along the beach or on the pier.

Day trips from Melbourne

There is plenty to see in Victoria, even though it is such a small state. The **VLine** (Victoria's train system) or the organised day tours can take you to many places.

You might wish to step back in time to the goldrush days at **Sovereign Hill** and pan for gold. Or witness the recreation of the battle of the Eureka Stockade at **Ballarat**.

You could take a walk in the **Grampians**, take a paddlesteamer cruise along the **Murray River** or head to bushranger country in **Glenrowan**.

Surfers will want to check out **Bell's Beach** and catch a wave or two.

Maybe visit **Hanging Rock** for a picnic.

Take a day tour to see the **Twelve Apostles**, spectacular rock formations on the coast.

Tasmania is often forgotten on people's travels. To get there you can either take a flight or take the overnight ride across the Tasman Sea on the luxurious *Spirit of Tasmania* from Melbourne to **Launceston**.

You could purchase a 7, 14 or 30-day bus pass and tour around the island yourself, take an organised tour, or hire a car. Visit the coastal features of **Tasman's Arch** and **Devil's Kitchen** before reaching the historic penal settlement at **Port Arthur**, which gives you an insight into the life endured by the convicts.

In **Hobart** on the Derwent River try your luck at the **Wrest Point Casino**, the first casino in Australia, or go to the top of **Mount Wellington** for a view over the city and the harbour.

Drop into Australia's **Antarctic Research Headquarters**.

Visit the **Huon Valley**, see the **Apple Museum** and sample some apple butter spread.

See the alpine scenery at **Cradle Mountain** which is part of the World Heritage Wilderness area. You might spot a Tasmanian Devil. Experience the **Franklin-Gordon Wild Rivers National Park** and cruise **Lake Gordon**. Tour the underground power station complex of **Gordon Dam**. Or maybe go white water rafting on the **Franklin River**, saved from damming by the greenies and also the place where the Wilderness Society first began.

Back in Melbourne, take the **Great Ocean Road** which is a must. If you're heading to Adelaide you may like to take the **Wayward Bus** which travels back and forth between these two cities.

This coastline is spectacular, with the natural wonders of the **Twelve Apostles**, **London Bridge**, the **Otway Ranges** and tales of shipwrecks.

At **Warrnambool**, watch for Southern right whales. Then on to Adelaide.

Adelaide is known as the City of Churches. It is easy to walk as the streets are well planned-out over a square mile grid and are surrounded by parkland. If you don't want to walk you could take the hop-on hop-off **Adelaide Explorer** tram.

You might want to wander through the museums or along the **Torrens River**. Visit the **Town Hall**, **Victoria Square**, **St. Peter's Cathedral** and the **Adelaide Oval**. Do some shopping at **Rundle Mall**. Perhaps take a tram to the seaside at **Glenelg** to sit on the beach or see **HMS** *Buffalo*.

Take a day trip to the **Barossa Valley** to taste some wines. Don't forget to go to **Mengler's Hill Lookout** for a view over the valley.

Go to **Hahndorf**, the oldest German settlement in Australia, to browse through the craft shops or eat some German food on the main street.

Visit **Victor Harbour**, once a whaling town and now a popular holiday resort with a horse-drawn tram to **Granite Island**. Maybe see some whales.

Take a break on **Kangaroo Island**. See the native wildlife and walk amongst the sea lions at **Seal Bay**.

From Adelaide to Perth it's a good 35 hours on the bus, across the **Nullarbor** and along the Eyre Highway. Much of the highway hugs the coastal cliffs overlooking the **Great Australian Bight**, so get a seat on the left side of the bus (or right side if you are travelling from Perth to Adelaide).

The first town at the end of the highway (nearly 2000 km away from Adelaide) is **Norseman**, known as the Golden Gate to the Western State. It is named after the horse Norseman who scratched the ground and found a gold nugget.

From Norseman, head north to the twin towns of **Kalgoorlie** and **Boulder** to see Australia's largest gold mine. You might even gain some work there. From here it's a long 8–10 hour drive through flat farming country to Perth.

Perth is the capital of Western Australia. Most people stay in **Northbridge**, a vibrant part of town with many restaurants and within easy walking distance of the commercial side of town.

You may like to take the **Perth Tram Explorer** and hop on and off at the sights of your choice.

Everyone goes to **Kings Park** with its natural bush setting for panoramic views over the city.

You may like to take a cruise on the **Swan River**, along which Perth is built.

Spend a day in **Fremantle** which is situated on the mouth of the Swan River. You can catch the sightseeing tram to tour the highlights.

Walk along the waterfront to see the yachts in the harbour, the place where Australia defended the America's Cup in 1987. Visit the **Maritime Museum**, the **Fremantle Prison** and the **Round House**.

Another day take a cruise out to **Rottnest Island** and see the quokkas.

If you just want to laze in the sun there are some beautiful beaches.

Further afield from Perth

There is a lot to see in Western Australia and many of the sights are long distances from Perth.

To get around Western Australia you might wish to find out about Westrail passes, take some day trips by bus, or hire a car.

You might wish to visit **Wave Rock** around 350 km south-east of Perth. The rock has been shaped like a wave by wind and rain and is believed to be around 2700 million years old. A short walk away is **Hippo's Yawn**. It is a long way just to see the rock so you might consider heading south to **Esperance**, known as the Bay of Islands, then follow the road west to **Albany**. There are some beautiful beaches along this coastline and you could do some whale watching.

From Perth you could head south to **Bunbury** where dolphins come into **Koombana Bay** to swim. Keep heading south along the **Caves Road** and stop in to see the caves, especially **Jewel Caves** which are spectacular. Continuing south you can go to **Cape Leeuwin** and see where the Great Southern Ocean meets the Indian Ocean.

Heading north from Perth visit the **Pinnacles Desert** to see the limestone spires. Continue up towards **Shark Bay** to **Monkey Mia** (which is a good day's drive) to interact with the dolphins. From here, head back to Perth or over the top to Darwin.

8 Useful information

Aboriginal Australia—Aborigines have inhabited Australia for over 40,000 years. Few other Australians or visitors know or understand much about their culture because their history has never been written down. What we do think about are their paintings, their dancing, their food, their didgeridoo playing and their Dreamtime.

You won't see many Aborigines, or Kooris as they prefer to be called, in the major cities as they mostly live in the outback areas of the Northern Territory, northern Queensland and Western Australia.

Land rights are a big issue in Australia. In 1992 the High Court passed a ruling which set aside the annexation of Australia as *Terra Nullius* (empty land). This acknowledged that the Aborigines were the first inhabitants of this land, whose rights to their laws and lands had not been extinguished. Claims for land to be handed back to the original owners are in progress.

ANZAC Day—Commemorated on 25 April each year, this is a day of remembrance for the Australian and New Zealand diggers (soldiers) killed in the wars. (ANZAC stands for Australian and New Zealand Army Corps).

There are dawn services and marches all over the country followed by games of two-up (the only day it is legally allowed to be played) and drinks with mates at RSL (Returned Soldiers' League) clubs.

Aussie tucker—British fare was brought by white settlers to these shores so roast lamb, beef or chicken dinners, fish and chips and scones with jam and cream are on the menu.

Bushmen invented damper bread and billy tea.

Other tucker includes lamingtons, neenish tarts, pavlova, Vegemite, Paddle Pops, Cherry Ripes, Violet Crumbles, meat pies and sauce, witchetty grubs, kangaroo, crocodile, macadamia nuts, Iced Vovos, Chicko Rolls, hamburgers with salad, beetroot and barbecue sauce—I'm sure you'll enjoy finding out for yourself what they taste like.

As Australia is very multicultural there are a lot of cuisines around to try.

There are **backpacker scenes** in most places. In the capital cities there are pubs that are popular and even have backpacker nights. Ask at the hostels for information if you want to get into the scene. Some hostels even have pub crawl buses.

In Sydney pick up a copy of the free magazine, *Beat*, from post offices and hostels—it lists what's on and details the nightlife. Most newspapers also have gig guides.

Bank opening times are 9.30 am to 4 pm Monday to Thursday, 9.30 am to 5 pm on Fridays and some are open on Saturdays. Watch out for pension days when it can be very busy. ATMs can be used at any time.

Barbecues are a popular pastime. If you are invited to one the norm is to BYO meat and grog (alcohol). The host/hostess supplies the salads and some soft drink.

Don't be surprised if the males hover around the barbie to advise the host on how to barbecue while the females offer the hostess help in the kitchen. Usually the hostess has everything under control, so the girls can socialise or laugh at the men barbecuing.

Redheads shouldn't be offended if called **blue/bluey**—it's just a nickname.

Bushfires are a regular occurrence in hot weather and unfortunately some are lit deliberately. To help reduce their severity, controlled burns are undertaken during the winter months.

Watch out for bushfire alerts. Entrances to national parks will show the fire danger and it is mentioned during weather reports.

If you are camping make sure your fire is extinguished by throwing dirt on it. Don't throw cigarette butts out of car windows.

If there is a fire and you are in your car, find an open area off the road (in case fire engines come blazing through), stay in the car, wind up the windows, close the air vents, get below window level, cover yourself and wait until the fire passes. Don't touch any metal as it might be hot; use a piece of material to open the door.

It is preferable to evacuate early if you are travelling on foot.

Bushrangers per se do not exist but during the late 1800s they roamed Australia, leaving a legacy as folk heroes. Ned Kelly is Australia's most famous bushranger. See his death mask, armour and where he was hanged at the Melbourne Gaol, or the site of his last gun battle in Glenrowan, Victoria.

Clothes—Dressing in Australia is of a casual nature. During hot weather most people wear cool loose fitting, shorts and t-shirts, dresses, etc.

City people do dress differently from country folk who favour jeans, shirts, Akubra hats and Driza-Bones.

The **currency** is simple and based on the decimal system of 100 cents to the dollar.

The one and two cent coins have been phased out but things can still cost, say, 98c. When this happens the price is either rounded up or down to the nearest 5 cents.

The silver coins are the 5c, 10c, 20c and 50c pieces. Then there are the gold $1 and $2 coins.

Papers notes have been phased out and are replaced with polymer notes which are the pinky purple $5 note, the blue $10 note, the orange $20 note, the gold $50 note and in 1996 the grey $100 note. All the notes honour famous Australians.

Most shopkeepers don't like receiving $50 or $100 notes if you are buying something small as it can take all their change.

Cyclones are common in the summer months in tropical North Queensland, the Northern Territory and the northern region of Western Australia.

If one is heading your way get right out of town or stay indoors. Find the smallest room in the house, take provisions and have a torch.

Dates are written with the day first, then the month, then the year.

Australia has some of the ***deadliest creatures*** in the world.
- *Bees*—Those lovely little critters that make our honey can cause an allergic reaction in some. If you're stung remove the sting by scraping it out, clean the wound and apply a cold compress. Seek medical help if and allergic reaction occurs.
- *Wasps*—Unlike bees, wasps often sting several times. Isn't that nice of them? They are attracted to sweet drinks and meat being cooked so watch out for them at those barbies. Apply a cold compress and seek medical help if an allergic reaction occurs.
- *Blue-ringed octopus*—You'll find this octopus living in rock pools on the beach. They are harmless when left alone but if they're disturbed vivid blue rings appear on their skin. A bite from one of these can be fatal so seek medical help urgently. It is advisable to leave them alone.
- *Cone shells*—Those shells you often pick up while walking on reefs may be cone shells. They have deadly stingers which come out the bottom of the shell. If you're stung pour vinegar over the sting and

seek medical help.
- *Crocodiles* There are two types of crocodile, the saltwater and freshwater. Both are found in Far North Queensland and the Northern Territory. Salties (saltwater) are very dangerous. Freshies (freshwater) are harmless if left alone, so they say, though I wouldn't trust them.

    I've heard that if one comes at you you should run away in a zigzag pattern because they can't run that way—I haven't tested this theory out and I don't plan to.
- *Sharks* There are sharks all around the coastline of Australia. They like to feed during sunrise and sunset.

    Most patrolled beaches have shark nets to keep them out and an alarm will go off to get everyone out of the water if one is spotted. Helicopters will often come in to herd it/them back out to sea.

    If you're worried about them, swim in the waves close to the beach. They don't come into the shallows as sand gets into their gills—poor darlings.

    If a shark comes at you hit it on the nose as apparently that's their vulnerable spot. I haven't tested this theory out either.

    If you're bitten, stem the flow of blood by applying pressure to the wound and seek medical help.
- *Snakes* are more scared of us than we are of them, so if you encounter one, stand still or back away slowly.

    It is against the law to run over them on purpose if you see one slithering on the road.

    If you are bitten take note of what it looks like so the correct antivenom can be given. Don't suck out or wash off the venom as if you don't recognise what type of snake bit you, the venom will help in identifying it. Immobilise the entire limb with a pressure bandage and splint, and seek medical advice.
- *Spiders* are all over Australia.

    Funnel Webs can be found around Sydney, found on the NSW coast and in south-east Queensland. I strongly advise you not to go looking for them as their bite is very painful and deadly. They are big spiders about 2 or 3 cm in length—well, I call that big—and are black or reddish brown. If bitten, seek urgent medical attention.

    Redback spiders are identifiable by the red markings on their back. They are small black spiders with a big bite and live in most parts of Australia. Give boots and gloves a shake before you put them on. When camping, check your sleeping bag before you get in.
- *Stingers/jellyfish/blue bottles* All these creatures are predominantly found in coastal waters during the warmer months. Their stings can cause great pain and leave welts on the skin. If possible, flood the sting with vinegar as that neutralises the tentacles enough for you to gen-

tly pick them off. Applying ice can relieve the pain. Seek medical help.
- *Stonefish*—Watch out for these while walking in shallow tropical waters. As the name suggests they look like stones but are actually fish with very painful, poison-bearing spikes on their back. Wear shoes or thongs when wading in water. If you step on a stonefish, remove the spikes and seek medical help.
- *Ticks* live all over Australia. They are either oval or round and flat but when engorged with blood they increase in size. They hide in body crevices or in your hair and can cause paralysis. Pull them out with tweezers and seek medical advice if you find any on your body.

A ***departure tax*** is required to leave Australia but as of 1 July 1995 it has been included in the price of your ticket.

Drinking—To drink alcohol in licensed premises you must be over 18.

There are a variety of beers available; some have full strength alcohol content and others are light (low alcohol content).

Beers on tap are served in a glass. Glasses vary in size and can be called different names. For example, a 'schooner' in NSW is known as a 'pot' in Queensland. You can also buy 'middies'. If you're unsure of the size just ask for a beer and the bar person will usually pick up a glass and say 'This size?' You don't have to return a glass to be refilled as you are given a new glass for each drink.

Beer can also be bought as a 'tinnie' or 'tube' which means in the can. It's a little uncouth for girls to drink from a can—besides, I think it tastes different.

You can also buy beer in bottles of varying sizes. Most are 'twisties', meaning capped with a twist top. Don't use your teeth to open them.

If you are having a party you can buy a keg.

Beers are served ice-cold. After a long hot day you'll know why. Be careful not to leave your finger tips or lips behind on the glass.

Each state produces its own beer, such as Swan Lager in WA, in NSW—Tooheys, in Victoria—VB (Victorian Bitter), and in Queensland it's XXXX, but there are new beers hitting the market all the time. If you like beer you'll enjoy trying them.

You can find a drink in pubs, RSL clubs, Leagues clubs, trade union clubs (you may have to join the clubs and dress nicely, including shoes), nightclubs and restaurants.

Alcohol cannot be bought at supermarkets; it must be bought from a licensed bottle shop. These are often attached to pubs where you can obtain drive-through service.

Pubs also serve counter meals which are good value. On Friday nights they often have raffles with meat trays, vegetables and chooks (chickens) on offer for prizes.

Many pubs have beer gardens which are nice to sit in with a cold drink or a meal on a warm day.

Drivers follow the left-hand side of the road. There are many roads around Australia, the major ones being sealed. Minor roads can have a dirt surface. Some roads have a single lane of tar seal, and when a car approaches from the other direction you will need to move off the seal to pass each other. Many roads are named after explorers.

Speed limits are in kilometres. In built-up areas you can do 60 km an hour, in school zones 40 km and on the open road 100 km an hour. There are road signs to tell you the speed, but speeds can vary from State to State. For example, in the Northern Territory you can only do 25 km an hour in public places or off-street carparks.

For those who might have bought an old car which only shows miles on the speedometer, convert your speed to kilometres by using this rough formula: divide miles by five, then multiply by eight to get kilometres. Here's an example: you're driving 50 miles an hour, divide by five = 10, then multiply by eight = 80 km per hour. To save your brain, 60 km = 37.5 miles; 40 km = 25 miles; and 100 km = 62.5 miles .

It is compulsory to wear a seatbelt in both the front and back seats.

If you drive with one arm leaning out the window put suntan lotion on it, or wear a long sleeved shirt.

It is polite when stuck behind a slow vehicle on a single lane road to let the car immediately behind the slow vehicle overtake first, though there is usually some jerk who speeds up and around everyone else. Also only overtake on straight stretches of road, not on corners.

If someone flashes their lights at you it usually means something is wrong with your own lights, or that there are police ahead. It is illegal to advise others that police are ahead but people still do it.

Watch out for roundabouts. The main rule is to give way to the right and only enter when it is clear. If you are turning left or going straight through stay in the left lane. If you're turning right stay in the right lane.

When driving long distances, make sure you have adequate rest breaks and if possible share the driving.

When driving, don't overtake on double lines, and watch out for: toll ways; pot holes; road trains; speed humps; wildlife crossings; bugs splattering on windscreens; petrol running low; scenic drives; tourist attractions; cattle crossings; cattle grids; closed gates; speed cameras; railway level crossings (not protected by boom barriers or warning lights—slow down); hairpin bends; slow drivers; tourist buses on narrow roads; workmen; bikes; high wind areas; road signs—slippery when wet, speed limits, school areas and bus loading zones; accident zones;

fatigue zones; falling rocks; flood areas; dirt roads—when passing cars on a dirt road you might wish to put your hand against the windscreen to help absorb the shock of flying stones; quarantine bins at state borders to throw fruit and vegetables in.

Don't drink and drive as there are stiff penalties. Your blood alcohol level must stay under 0.05 ml of alcohol per 100 ml of blood; and if in a rental car, under 0.02 ml. Random breath testing units, known as booze buses, can appear anywhere.

Road rules can vary from state to state, including the speed limit so pick up a set of *Interstate Road Rules* from a motor authority.

Driving in the outback—Make sure your vehicle is prepared for the outback. Have it fully checked over before setting out. Take spare tyres, food, plenty of water and fuel and if you break down stay with the vehicle. Off the main road, property owners never ignore smoke—burn a tyre maybe. If you are going really off-road advise someone, such as the police or the hostel, where you are going and when you'll arrive.

Motoring organisations have information available to their members about driving in the outback and equipping the car for such trips. Ask for information when you obtain maps, etc. from them.

If you are planning to go off-road find out if you will be travelling through *Aboriginal land*, because you will need a special permit to enter the area. Tours have this special permission.

Eating out—Backpackers rarely dine out; it's a good cheap feed you're after. Spending about A$4–10 a meal is the norm.

Look out for cafes and BYO restaurants. Food halls in shopping centres have a variety of cheap eateries. The corner milk bar makes hamburgers, fish and chips, etc. RSL clubs, trade union clubs and football clubs all have restaurants which serve good meals. You may have to join one of them, but it might be worth it to get a decent feed.

Australia is a very multicultural country so there are a lot of cuisines to try including Chinese, Thai, Japanese, Mexican, Indian, etc.

All the fast food chains like McDonald's, Pizza Hut, KFC, etc. offer a cheap meal.

There are 'cheap eat' books available if you are serious about eating lots at little cost.

Ask your hostel to recommend a place.

Eating well while travelling—One thing that lapses while travelling is putting nutritious food into your body. I know it can be easy to eat at fast food joints every night but do try and eat correctly.

Eating cheaply while travelling is another concern, unless there are a few of you who can split the bill and cook a meal.

Instead of buying a drink at every stop, you can fill up your water

bottle and drink that. Then splurge out now and again.
Take your own plastic knife, fork and spoon.
Take your own jar of coffee.

Eucalyptus oil is highly flammable which is why the Australian bush, having so many eucalyptus trees, is highly combustible.

In an **emergency** dial 000 for the Police, Ambulance or Fire Brigade.

Native **fauna** includes koalas, kangaroos, wallabies, wombats, platypuses, bilbies, possums, quokkas, echidnas and dingos. There are many birds including the kookaburra, emu and a range of parrots and cockatoos. They can be seen in zoos, wildlife parks or better still, in their native environment.

Flies can be annoying creatures. They especially like hanging around at barbecues. Watch out for the big blowies.

There is an active **gay scene**. In Sydney pick up a copy of the free fortnightly *Sydney Star Observer*. Many clubs and pubs are located along Oxford Street, known as the 'golden mile'. You might want to ring the gay What's On hot-line.
Tasmania is the only state in Australia with prohibitive legislation outlawing homosexual activity though many are championing the gay cause in order to change this.

The **heat and humidity** can affect people in different ways. Drink plenty of water or energy drinks if you feel washed out. Try and stay cool. Sunstroke can occur when your body's heat regulating system breaks down and you fail to sweat.

Lingo (language) is quite unique. Many words have letters not pronounced, or words have been shortened, e.g.:

ace	excellent
'ang on	wait a minute
arvo	afternoon
Aussie	Australian
'avago	have a go
banana bender	a person from Queensland
barbie	barbecue
barra	barramundi (a type of fish)

barrack	supporting your team (don't say 'root'; in Oz, this is an expression for having sex)
beyond the black stump/ back of Bourke	a remote area
bickie	biscuit
blowie	blow fly
bludger	lazy person
blue heeler	police officer or cattle dog
bonnet	hood of a car/truck, etc.
bonza	good, great
boot	trunk of a car
booze bus	police breath testing unit
bottleshop	off licence, alcohol shop
(you've got) Buckley's	you've got no chance
give it a burl	give it a go
(I'm) bushed	I'm tired
BYO/G	bring your own/grog
capsicum	peppers
cark it	die
chemist	drug store/pharmacy
chewy	chewing gum
chook	chicken
chuck a U-ee	do a U-turn
chunder/chuck/spew	vomit
clobber	clothes
cobber	friend (rarely used nowadays)
cocky	farmer, or cockatoo
come a cropper	have an accident
cooee	a bush call
cop	police officer
cossies	bathing costume
crash/doss	sleep
crow eater	a South Australian
dag	untidy or unfashionable person
daks/strides	trousers
dead set	really, truly, genuine
derro	tramp/homeless person
digger/s	Australian soldier/s
dinky-di	genuine
doona	duvet
drongo	idiot
duco	car paint
dunny/loo	outside toilet

Useful information

durex	in England it's sticky-tape, in Oz, it's a condom
earbash	talk a lot
eggplant	aubergine
esky	a portable cooling box
fair crack of the whip	fair go
fair dinkum	really, truly, genuinely
fair enough	that's OK, acceptable
fair go	a reasonable chance
ferals	people living 'at one' with nature
football	Rugby League, Rugby Union, AFL
Fremantle Doctor	the sea breeze in Perth
galah	a bird, or a loud, noisy person
garbo	garbage collector
full as a goog	drunk
get the guernsey	be the winner
gladwrap	cling film
good-o	OK
greenie	conservationist
grog/plonk/booze/piss	alcohol
G'day	hello
had a gutful	had enough
hock	sell or pawn
jig	play truant
Kiwi	person from New Zealand
liquid paper	white-out
loaded	wealthy or drunk
go to the local	go to the pub
lollies	sweets
main street/main drag	high street
mate	good friend
Mexican	someone south of the border—Queenslanders call NSW people Mexicans and NSW people call Victorians Mexicans
middie	medium-sized glass of beer
mollydooker	left-handed person
mozzie	mosquito
mug	fool
nick off/rack off/get lost	go away
no worries	no problem
the norm	the normal or regular thing to do
in the nuddy/starkers	in the nude or naked
OS (gone)	gone overseas

Oz	Australia
pokies	poker machines
postcode	zip code
postie	postman or mailman
petrol	gas
prang	minor car accident
rego	car registration, MOT, road tax
sandgroper	someone from Western Australia
sangers	sandwiches
schooner/pot	large glass of beer
scorcher	hot day
scungies, dick-stickers	speedos, men's swimwear
shonky	poor quality or slightly illegal
sickie (take a)	a day off from work when not sick
smoko	a brief break from work
snags	sausages
southpaw	left-handed person
speedos	men's swimwear
spunky	good-looking
stinger	animal or plant that stings—e.g. jellyfish, blue bottle etc.
strewth	gee whiz
Strine	short for Australian (language)
tinnie/tube	can of beer
top drop	a good beer or wine
trendie	person who follows the trends
trots	races (usually harness/horse races), or it can mean diarrhoea
truckie	truck driver
true-blue	genuine
tucker	food
two-up	illegal gambling game where two coins are tossed in the air and bets taken on whether they land heads or tails
vacuum cleaner	hoover
wag	play truant
wally	idiot
walkabout	disappear for a while
whinge	complain or whine
whopper	a lie, or something larger than usual such as a wave
wobbly (chuck a)	have a temper tantrum, get upset
wog/wop	foreigner (derogatory term)

yakka	hard work
yobbo	uncultured person
yonks	ages ago/a long time
Yowie	fictional abominable snowman or bigfoot
yuppie	young urban professional person
zucchini	courgettes

There is short-term *luggage storage* available at airports as well as at major bus and train terminals. Your bags are usually kept in lockers which are often cleared daily.

Companies such as ITAS and Traveller's Contact Point do provide long-term luggage storage. See them for rates.

Some hostels will even look after luggage as a guarantee that you will return to stay with them once again.

Australia runs on the *metric* system. Speed and distance are measured in kilometres (km); temperature is in degrees Celsius (°C); weight is in kilograms (kg).

The only national *newspaper* is *The Australian.* Each state has its own paper/papers. There are also local papers plus an increasing number of Australian-produced ethnic newspapers.

To find out about the *nightlife* papers carry gig guides advertising which bands are playing, theatres, movies, etc.

Australia is the place to enjoy the great *outdoors* and there are plenty of activities to keep you occupied including: abseiling, ballooning, bungee jumping, bushwalking, hang-gliding, horseriding, white water rafting, cycling, sailing, scuba diving, snorkelling, skydiving, canoeing, rock climbing, surfing and my personal favourite, lying on a beach.

Politics/Government is based on the British system. Queen Elizabeth II is the official head of state with her representative in Australia being the Governor-General. Head of Parliament is the Prime Minister. There are three levels of government, Federal, State and Local.

Voting is compulsory for all Australians, who are fined if they don't vote.

Post is delivered Mondays to Fridays in populated areas by trusty posties on foot, on pushbikes, or motorbikes or in vans. In some remote areas deliveries might only be made once a week and could be by plane.

Post offices are open from 9 am to 5 pm. Sydney's General Post

Office is also open on Saturday mornings.

Local mail is usually delivered the next day. Interstate mail will take 1–2 days. At the time of publication it cost 45c to send a letter anywhere in Australia. You can buy *Express Post* satchels which guarantee next-day delivery anywhere in Australia.

To address a letter within Australia:
Name
Street No. then Street Name
Suburb State Postcode

The correct postcode is vital because if you get the suburb name wrong it will still get to the right place with a correct postcode.

State names are abbreviated, and each state's four-digit postcode begins with a different number:

Australian Capital Territory *and*	ACT	2
New South Wales	NSW	2
Northern Territory *and*	NT	5
South Australia	SA	5
Queensland	QLD	4
Tasmania	TAS	7
Victoria	VIC	3
Western Australia	WA	6

Public holidays

1st January	New Year's Day
26th January	Australia Day
Easter	March/April
25th April	ANZAC Day
12th June	Queen's Birthday (except WA)
October	Labour Day
25th December	Christmas Day
26th December	Boxing Day

Each state has various holidays.

There are many **radio stations** ranging from talk-backs, to commercial stations to the youth network of JJJ catering to many tastes. Twist the dial until you find something you like.

Most **religions** are catered for, though Australia is predominantly Church of England (Episcopal) or Catholic. Most townships have a church or two.

Shopping hours are mostly 9 am to 5.30 pm Mondays to Fridays with late night shopping on Thursdays in some areas. In areas that specifically cater to tourists like the Gold Coast shops will stay open most week-nights. They also open on a Saturday, usually till 4 pm though some small places close around noon. There is also Sunday trading in some areas.

You might find a bargain at the markets. In Sydney visit Paddy's Markets in Haymarket or Glebe markets.

Things to buy include Aboriginal art; a didgeridoo; lambs' wool; pottery and cottage crafts; a Driza-Bone coat; an Akubra hat and opals—or dig for your own at Coober Pedy.

There is no sales tax added on to the things you purchase as everything has tax already incorporated into the price.

Smoking is banned on all domestic flights, on public transport and in most buildings—that's why you see workers out the front of their buildings puffing away. Restaurants usually have a non-smoking and a smoking section.

Sunburn—When you're from a country not used to constant outdoor living you might overdose in the great outdoors. Sunburn is extremely painful. Like any burn you need to take the heat out of it. Soak yourself in a cool bath and apply liberal amounts of moisturiser. If you are burned badly enough to blister, seek medical attention.

Australia has the highest incidence of **skin cancer** in the world and even though you might have a desire to lie on every beach along Australia's coastline, be sensible about it.

Make sure you rub in suntan lotion with a sun protection factor (SPF) of 15+. Put it on at least half an hour before you go to the beach so it absorbs into your skin. Even if it is water-resistant, you should re-apply it after swimming as you can burn more easily in the water.

Also wear a wide-brimmed hat and sunglasses to protect your eyes. It is preferable to cover up completely.

Stay out of the sun during the hottest hours of the day—from 10 am to 2 pm (during daylight saving 11 am to 3 pm), as those nasty burning rays are at their strongest during these times.

Even though it looks healthy to have a tan you don't have to be the brownest berry around or you may end up a wrinkly old berry.

Social events for the calendar—There are too many events happening throughout the country at any one time to list them all but some of the major ones are:

- *January:* Festival of Sydney; Australia Day (26th); Australian Tennis Open in Melbourne; Tamworth Country Music Festival—a time for some real good ol' toe tapping, lasts for 10 days and culminates

in the Country Music Awards; Big Day Out—loads of local and international bands playing their way around the country.
- *February:* Gay and Lesbian Mardi Gras—not to be missed; Chinese New Year.
- *March:* Melbourne's Moomba Festival; Adelaide Arts Festival; Royal Easter Show in Sydney; Indy Grand Prix on the Gold Coast; Comedy Festival in Melbourne lasting 10 days; Formula I Grand Prix in Melbourne.
- *April:* ANZAC Day (25th); Surfing competition at Bell's Beach, Victoria.
- *May:* Adelaide Cup; Camel Cup in Alice Springs.
- *June:* Sydney Film Festival—two weeks of movies at various venues; Ski season begins.
- *July:* Darwin Beer Can Regatta.
- *August:* New Year's Eve ski season; City-to-Surf foot race, Sydney.
- *September:* Bathurst 1000—car race on the Mount Panorama Circuit; Winter sport finals; Birdsville Races.
- *October:* Henley-on-Todd Regatta, Alice Springs; Cricket season begins; Sleaze Ball; Iron man series, running throughout the summer, begins.
- *November:* Melbourne Cup (first Tuesday).
- *December:* Carols by candlelight; Boxing Day, the beginning of the Sydney-to-Hobart Yacht Race—stand on the headlands or on the beaches along the coast and watch the yachts on the way to Tasmania; NSW Tennis Open—White City, Sydney.

The **Southern Cross** is a constellation only seen in the southern hemisphere and is on the Australian national flag. It is sometimes called the 'saucepan'.

Sporting mad—Australia has many sporting codes. The major spectator sports are cricket in summer and Rugby League, Rugby Union and AFL (known as 'Aussie Rules') in winter.

There is plenty of sport on TV if you can't make it to the actual ground. Many pub TVs have a sports program on, so a possible conversation starter could be: 'What's the score?'

Cricket is the only game played in every state while Aussie Rules football is mostly popular in Victoria, Tasmania, South Australia and Western Australia. Rugby League and Rugby Union are popular in Queensland and New South Wales.

If you're eating out, and find **surf and turf** on the menu, expect a meal of seafood and meat.

The *tax* year runs from 1 July to 30 June each year. At the end of each year you have until the end of October to submit a tax return. Working holidaymakers must lodge a tax return either after 30 June or before they leave.

Only residents of Australia receive a tax-free threshold. Non-residents (working holidaymakers) do not. The tax you pay is the tax you owe.

You are not entitled to a rebate, but you might receive a tax credit which you can include in your tax return in your home country.

Some accountants do advise you to tick the resident box when you're not actually resident so you can obtain a rebate. BUT if instead of a rebate you owe the tax department, you will have to pay. Many holidaymakers don't pay up and leave town, but the tax department has reciprocal arrangements with some countries. After a few years, when the interest has increased the amount you owe, they can trace you and demand that you pay it. If you don't, it can affect your chances of ever coming back to Australia.

If you want to know more about tax laws in Australia, contact the Tax Department.

Using the *telephone system* is easy. Calls can be made from private phones or public phones.

Public phones take money, phonecards, EFTPOS cards or credit cards.

Local calls costs 25c from a private phone and 40c from a public phone and the good thing is, you can natter as long as you like, though the person waiting to use the phone won't be too pleased. Good manners suggest you limit calls on public phones to 3 minutes if someone else is waiting. Coins accepted include 10c, 20c, 50c and $1 coins. Phonecards can be purchased from newsagents in various denominations. When using your EFTPOS card money will be debited from your account, or charged to a credit card.

Using the phone is easy. For money and phonecard phones, lift the handset, put your money or phonecard in the appropriate spots and when you hear the dial tone, dial your number.

When using EFTPOS and credit card phones, lift the handset and swipe your card, select your account (i.e. cheque, savings, credit), enter your PIN and when you hear the dial tone, dial your number.

With the increased use of fax machines, etc. Australia is running out of numbers. In 1994 a process began to restructure the system to provide enough numbers as the demand grows. Eventually, all numbers will have a two-digit area code and an eight-digit number.

Phone calls in Australia are either local, STD—long distance within Australia, or IDD—international.

Emergency calls	000
Directory assistance	013 (local) or 0175 (elsewhere)
Overseas directory assistance	0103

To *telephone outside Australia* with International Direct Dial, dial 0011—country code—area code—then the number.

Look out for cheap rates, these are usually available after 10 pm Monday to Saturday and all day Sunday. Before you call, work out the time difference first as you don't want to speak to a grumpy friend or relative.

You could always arrange to make reverse-charge calls once a month, and whomever you signed your power of attorney over to or authorised to operate your account could pay the bill from your funds.

Phones congregate around post offices, train stations, airports and bus terminals—some of the noisiest places.

Phone calls from hotel accommodation are more expensive than from public phones.

Australia has three **time zones**, Eastern Standard Time, Central Standard Time and Western Standard Time.

Eastern Standard Time covers the eastern states of Queensland, New South Wales, Victoria and Tasmania and is 10 hours ahead of Greenwich Mean Time.

Central Standard Time covers South Australia and the Northern Territory and is 30 minutes behind Eastern Standard Time. So it is 9½ hours ahead of Greenwich Mean Time

Western Standard Time covers all of Western Australia and is two hours behind Eastern Standard Time, 1½ hours behind Central Standard Time and 8 hours ahead of Greenwich Mean Time. Confused? Well, during summertime, some states have daylight saving just to confuse you even more.

New South Wales, Victoria, the ACT and South Australia have daylight saving which usually begins on the last Sunday in October and ends the first Sunday in March. Tasmania also has daylight saving but begins it on the last Sunday in October and ends the last Sunday in March.

Daylight saving gives those states that have it an extra hour's daylight which means it stays light well into the evening. Clocks are turned back an hour so Western Standard Time becomes only 1 hour behind Eastern Standard Time and half an hour behind Central Standard Time.

If you ever wanted to celebrate two New Years' Eves, now's your chance. Have one in New South Wales, then cross the border and celebrate again an hour later in Queensland.

Tipping is discretionary. If you thought the service was really good you might want to tip about 10% of the bill, or leave the change behind.

Taxi drivers are appreciative when you round up the fare.

There are 5 main *TV channels*. Two, the ABC (Australian Broadcasting Corporationy) and SBS (which transmits many foreign language films), are government funded networks.

The commercial networks include Channels 7, 9 and 10. Not all areas receive the channels.

A recent addition to Australian shores are Pay TV stations.

Water is safe to drink, though it doesn't always taste good. If you're worried about it, boil it.

The early 90s have seen Australia hit with the worst drought ever on record. If you find yourself in a drought-declared area, adhere to the water restrictions—you'll make yourself very unpopular, especially in country areas, if you ignore the restrictions.

Visa enquiries should be directed to the Department of Immigration. There are offices in major cities if you need them.

Sydney
88 Cumberland Street
The Rocks
Sydney NSW 2000

Weather varies from area to area and once you start watching weather forecasts you'll understand just how diverse the weather can be.

Australia has many *World Heritage-listed areas* including Kakadu and Uluru-Kata Tjuta National Parks in the Northern Territory, the Great Barrier Reef, the Wet Tropics and Fraser Island in Queensland, Rainforests and the Willandra Lakes Region in New South Wales, the Australian Mammal Fossil Sites in South Australia, Shark Bay in Western Australia and the Tasmanian Wilderness in Tasmania.

Respect them and enjoy them.

Index

Aboriginal Australia 140
Accommodation
    pre-book 26
    living in Sydney 55
    living in other parts 56
    long-term 52
    short-term 47
    when to go 11
Accounting positions 66
Agricultural positions 69
Airfares 12
Air miles 27
ANZAC 140
Arriving
    at other airports 42
    by sea vessel 39
    by air 39
    at Sydney airport 40
Au pair positions 75
Aussie tucker 140
Australian Tourist Commission 31

B&B 51
Backpacker scenes 141
Bank accounts
    open on arrival 43
    opening one from home 22
    opening times 141
Banking, finance, stockbroking 76
Barbecues 141
Barwork 77
Blue/bluey 141
Bondi 46
Bushfires 141
Bushrangers 141

Busking positions 78

Camping/caravan parks 51
Charity collecting positions 78
Check list 33
Child/elder carer positions 79
CMC 27
Computer contracting positions 80
Credit card 23
Currency 142
Customer sourcing positions 82
Cyclones 142

Dates, how written 142
Deadly creatures 142
Deck hand/cook positions 82
Departure tax 144
Diving instructor positions 84
Drinking 144
Driving 145
Duty-free 28

Eating out 146
Electronic voice-mail services 30
Emergency phone numbers 147
Eucalyptus oil 147

Farm/station work positions 85
Farm stays 51
Fauna 147
Flies 147

Gay scene 147
Glebe 46

Index

Heat and humidity 147
Holiday insurance 24
Hospitality positions 87
Hostels 47
    BRA 27, 50
    in Sydney 50
    YHA 27, 49

International driver's licence 27
ISIC 27

Journalism and photography 89

Learning English 58
Legal positions 90
Lingo 147
Luggage storage 151

Kings Cross 45

Magazines
    Aussie Backpacker 32
    TNT Travel Planner 32
    Go Australia 33
Mail holding/advisory service 28
Manly 46
Maps 43
Medical care
    Medicare 44
    reciprocal arrangements 25
Metric system 151
Money 22

Newspapers 151
Nightlife 151
Nursing positions 91

Office support positions 95
Outdoors 151

Packing 15
Particular events 13
Passport 10
Politics/Government 151
Possessions insurance 56
Post 151
Power of attorney 24
Public holidays 152

Radio stations 152
Religion 152
Resort work positions 99
Roadhouse positions 102

Scientific/lab staff positions 102
Shopping 152
Sightseeing
    Adelaide 138
    Brisbane 129
    Darwin 134
    Melbourne 136
    New South Wales 113
    Outback 133
    Perth 138
    rest of Australia 114, 127
    Sydney 107
        trips from Sydney 112
Skin cancer 153
Smoking 153
Social events 153
Southern Cross 154
Sport 154
Student visa 58
Street directory 43
Suggested routes
    Across the bottom 135
    East Coast 128
    Tasmania 137
    The outback 133
    To/from the outback 133
Sunburn 153
Surf and turf 154

Tax 155
    what's taken from salary 65
Tax file number 44
Teaching positions 103
Technical, industrial, trades, unskilled 104
Telephone system 155
Time zones 156
Tipping 157
Transport
    around Australia 116
    around Sydney 107
    from Sydney airport 43
Travel consultant positions 105
Travel

alone 34
  pre-book: passes and tours 26
  safe 35
  well 37
Travel centres
  who can organise 120
TV 157

Vaccinations 25
Visa enquiries 157

Waiting positions 106
Weather 157

  prime times to travel 11
Will: making one 24
World Heritage-listed areas 157
Work
  opportunities 57
  Studying and working 58
  through CES 61
  through hostels 64
  through temporary agencies 62
  when to go 13
  in Sydney and NSW 59
  in other states 59
Working holiday visa 9